Gaza:

Symbol of Resistance

Edited and compiled

by Joyce Chediac

D0757233

World View Forum

2011

GAZA: Symbol of Resistance

Edited by Joyce Chediac

ISBN 978 0 8956717 45 (paperback: alk. paper)
Copyright © 2011

Library of Congress Control Number: 2010942161

World View Forum
55 W. 17th St., 5th Floor
New York, N.Y. 10011

Cover art by Lal Roohk

Produced by Dee Knight

Table of Contents

Introduction

Why care about Gaza?

For those of us living in the United States, the plight of the people of the Gaza Strip matters, not only because of the great injustices done, but because we are forced to pay for the very weapons that bring misery to so many people there.

We are given no choice. In the name of fighting "terrorism," schools and hospitals are closed, services are cut and untold billions of dollars are spent making war throughout the Middle East. The same bankers who care not a whit about the suffering of the Palestinians care not a whit whether people in the U.S. have jobs, health care, schools and other necessities of life.

When we learn about Palestine, we learn about ourselves—how the very human thirst for justice and dignity is worldwide and cannot be wiped away no matter the odds.

Who are the people of Gaza?

More than a million of the 1.5 million Palestinians who live in Gaza are refugees or the descendants of refugees driven from their towns and villages in 1948 in what is now called Israel. For more than 60 years they have lived in Gaza, which is little more than a strip of sand and does not have the resources to support such a dense population. Their situation remains unresolved.

This writer was in Gaza in 1988, as a witness to the first Intifada. I spoke with families whose homes had been broken into by Israeli soldiers in the middle of the night in raids meant to terrorize. Young men and women showed me their scars and bruises from beatings by soldiers. I watched grandmothers, as a matter of course, risk their lives by running into the streets and wresting Palestinian youth from armed Israeli soldiers about to arrest them.

Living conditions in Gaza have always been difficult, and the level of struggle always high. But not like today.

Why read this book?

This book tells a compelling story. It begins in January 2006, when Hamas received an electoral majority from the Palestinian people, and ends shortly after May 31, 2010, when Israeli commandos attacked a flotilla of ships bringing humanitarian aid to Gaza and killed nine people.

Told here is how the impoverished Palestinian people in the tiny and resource-poor Gaza strip have withstood five years of siege, hunger, blockade and massive bombardment by Israel, but still stand tall, refusing to give up their right to determine their own lives and to choose their own government.

The world's most powerful governments sided with Israel, even while bombs rained down on Gaza civilians. The regimes in the U.S. and Europe participated in the economic strangulation of Gaza, and pretended not to see the suffering there.

People sickened and outraged at Gaza's punishment

But these governments did not speak for their people. From the U.S., Canada and Latin America to Europe, Asia and Africa, workers and progressives were sickened and outraged at the punishment of Gaza. The horror of the Israeli onslaught, the bravery of the Palestinians in Gaza, and the continued inaction of the big powers sparked actions in solidarity with Gaza across the globe.

A worldwide grassroots movement of organizations and individuals grew and began to defy the siege of Gaza and break the blockade by bringing in humanitarian aid themselves, even at the risk of their own lives.

Events revised by corporate media

Events in Gaza over those five years need to be told because even as they unfolded, the events were revised and distorted by the corporate media in Israel, the U.S. and Europe.

The victims—the Palestinian people and the Hamas government — were called the aggressors, while the true aggressor—the Israeli government backed and armed by Washington—was called the victim.

Solidarity activists who delivered humanitarian aid to Gaza at great risk were mostly ignored, with their stories, and sometimes their deaths, untold.

Hamas, Jewish opposition given a voice

This book fills in those gaps and sets the record straight. It also gives voice to those silenced by Fox News and the *New York Times*.

While there has been a great deal of invective in the corporate media about Hamas, these same newspapers and TV news shows have censored out Hamas's voice. This book includes what Hamas had to say in its own words about key events, about its motivation and about its goals.

Other Palestinians are given voice here. A Palestinian Marxist explains class relations in the Middle East. The questions "What do Palestinians want?" and "How can supporters best help?" are answered by a Palestinian leader in the U.S.

Many Jewish people, inside and outside of Israel, back Palestinian rights. They are sickened by the slaughter the Israeli state has committed in the false name of "protecting" them. Censored out of the main media, this book presents their views.

U.N. Goldstone report's findings detailed

The Goldstone Report was barely mentioned in the corporate media. This 574-page United Nations probe of the Gaza war is a scathing indictment of Israeli policy and war crimes. The report's Executive Summary is excerpted here, along with an exposé by Palestinian jurists of Israel's misuse of international law.

Many think that Israel is on one side and the Arabs are on the other. But this view does not consider that different social classes have different views. Here eyewitnesses document the Egyptian government's hostility to activists trying to enter Gaza with medicine. In marked contrast, the Egyptian people passionately oppose Gaza's strangulation. A Palestinian Marxist explains why this is so.

Provided here are the facts and analysis that answer: Who are the establishment media, and why don't they give the Palestinian people fair coverage? Why does the U.S. government always line up with Israel? Why have European and most U.S-aligned Arab regimes sat on their hands while Gaza burned and starves?

Gaza exposed imperialism's weakness

Many selections in this book refer to "imperialism." Imperialism is the current stage of capitalism. It is marked by the fusion of giant corporations with large banks to form finance capital. These U.S. and West European monopolies export capital to their neo-colonies to more efficiently plunder the resources and labor there, and increase their rate of profit at the colony's expense.

The U.S., the strongest imperial power, is the dominant force in the Middle East. So little Gaza is not up against just Israel, it is up against the U.S. and the whole predatory imperialist system.

This makes Gaza's courage even more important. By refusing to submit, Gaza has exposed the weakness of the whole imperialist system. While the U.S.-supplied high-tech weapons that Israel dropped on this small territory could kill and maim, they could not defeat a people united and determined to resist.

Gaza is still besieged

Gaza's ordeal has not ended. Its people are still besieged, and conditions there are harsh. It is hoped that this story of Gaza's resistance will move the reader to take some action in Gaza's behalf, and that this book provides the informational tools to explain to others why this is important.

Contributing writers have the highest credentials

Most of the material here has been reprinted or excerpted from *Workers World* newspaper, whose reporters worked diligently to tell the real story as the news broke by combing multiple news sources worldwide. Many writers also made fact-finding trips to the Middle East to report first-hand.

The contributors to this book are not political pundits who talk from their easy chairs. They are not reporters who go to the Middle East only to describe events from five-star hotels.

Some of the contributors to this book are Israeli or U.S. military resisters. Some have observed events in Palestine, Lebanon and elsewhere in the Middle East alongside the liberation struggles. Some have pushed through the blockade of Gaza at great personal risk to show solidarity, deliver aid and return with eyewitness reports. Some have organized the forums, the tribunals and the demonstrations that over the years make the true situation of the Palestinian people known.

They all have the very highest credentials: They are activists.

— Joyce Chediac, *editor, December 30, 2010*

Foreword

The following piece was written by Ramsey Clark, who was the U.S. attorney general during the Lyndon Johnson administration. Clark is an international law attorney, human rights advocate, and founder of the International Action Center. In his long career, Clark has worked with many heads of state.

For 30 years Clark was the attorney in the United States for the Palestine Liberation Organization. In that time he successfully litigated against attempts to close the P.L.O. Mission to the United Nations and stopped attempts to seize Palestinian assets in the U.S. He wrote this piece in January 2011, after leading a solidarity delegation to Gaza.

Here is the story of the most heroic and successful Palestinian resistance to unrelenting Israeli oppression and aggression, intended to drive the Palestinian people from their homeland, since 1948. It is a tale well told by authors with a wide range of personal backgrounds, knowledge, experience and perspectives, but a common commitment to a united, independent, free, secure and prosperous Palestinian nation and people. Their theme is the necessity of effective resistance to all forms of repression and aggression as essential to the freedom, dignity, and – with omni-destructive weapons and the environmental degradation that they cause – the survival of humanity.

The story of Gaza is twofold. On the one hand, the death and destruction that Gaza has suffered is tragic. On the other hand, Gaza's heroism and resistance is an inspiration which promises a strong, united Palestinian state.

Will of the Palestinian people ignored

The will of the Palestine people should determine who heads their government. Hamas received nearly 75 percent of the vote in the last Palestinian elections, despite all the handicaps imposed on it. Both Israel and the essential supporter of its belligerent and expansionist policies, the United States, profess to be and to esteem democracies. Yet both ignore the palpable will of the Palestinian people.

Israel, with U.S. cover, only dallies with Fatah while daily expanding its presence and power in the West Bank and Jerusalem. At the same time, Israel tightens its noose around Gaza, cutting off virtually all importation of human necessities. This blockade is spiced with bombings, shootings and political assassinations nearly daily.

A tale of two trips: Gaza in the 1990s and now

Representing the P.L.O. in U.S. courts for 30 years required close communication with Chairman, and later President, Yasser Arafat, and many trips to Palestine. Two of my trips to Gaza, one in the 1990s and one in January 2011, stand in marked contrast.

In the late 1990s, this crowded strip of land was brimming with a confident people. The streets were full of traffic. An airport was nearing completion. Schools and colleges were overflowing with students. Stores and pharmacies were full of goods. Restaurants were full of customers, good food and cheer. Government services and health care met basic needs. That was before the blockade, which began in 2006 and continues, and before the massive bombing of Gaza in 2008 to 2009.

In the 1990s, the drive from Cairo to Gaza and entry took four hours. In 2011 it took 19 hours.

The delay, deliberately caused by the Egyptian government, was designed to prevent or discourage entry. We left Cairo at 5:00 a.m. and could not enter Gaza until nearly 1:00 a.m. the next day. A large delegation had waited in Gaza since noon to meet us. When we finally arrived, they insisted on feeding us a dinner of scarce food, then taking us to a virtually empty Mediterranean beachfront hotel.

Gaza is about the size of Manhattan, Brooklyn and the Bronx combined, three boroughs of New York City. We drove the length and breadth of Gaza – 140 square miles. Rarely were we out of sight of destruction, damage and destitution, or a grim, if determined, adult population and their many cheerful children.

Hospitals are overflowing

Hospitals were full to overflowing with the injured and ill. There were severe shortages of life-saving medicines and medical equipment reminiscent of Iraq after the 1991 Gulf War. In Iraq, the sanctions killed more than were killed in the "shock and awe" invasion. One-and-a-half million Iraqis died as a result of sanctions, half of them children under the age of five. This is what Gaza faces now. Its hospitals are damaged, dialysis machines are broken – but it carries on.

Thousands of Palestinian prisoners are held in Israel, most often for purely political purposes. Many are from Gaza. Meetings with the parents, wives and children of prisoners was heart wrenching.

The greatest activity I saw in 2011 was education. It is booming even though many classrooms had been destroyed and there are near-daily military attacks on the strip, attacks which have included assassinations of civilian leadership and military personnel.

Meeting Hamas leadership

Much is said in the West about Hamas and the Hamas leadership, little of it good or accurate. A lengthy meeting and lunch with Prime Minister Ismail Haniyeh and members of his cabinet gave me great hope for Palestine's future. Haniyeh is a naturally cheerful man at 48, focused optimistically on the creation of a united Palestinian state that is free, independent and secure. More than grace under pressure, he showed knowledge, understanding, reasonableness, even a personal gentleness, and compassion.

Asked by many if Hamas plans a state in Gaza, Prime Minister Haniyeh has said: "We have no desire to establish a state in Gaza, particularly as its limited resources renders it unfit for statehood. And from a strategic, political and national perspective, we say, 'There can be no state in Gaza, and there can be no nation without it.' We have no desire to create a separate entity in the Strip, let alone a state."

Regarding an Islamic state, he has added, "It is impossible to define a nation before it has even been born because its identity is based on two factors: First, liberating the land and establishing a political entity upon it; and second, giving the people the right to present and choose. It is true we are Islamists, yet we respect our people's choices. If our citizenry choose an Islamic identity, we will work towards that; if they opt otherwise, we will equally understand and honor the people's voice."

I found the leadership of Hamas to be strong, committed to the unity of all Palestinians in their struggle for statehood, independence and freedom, and free from subversive influences that serve Israeli and U.S. policy. This leadership respects President Mahmoud Abbas and is open to work with him, consistent with the expressed will of the Palestinian people. It is the chosen leadership of the Palestinian people.

A world that believes in democracy must seek out Hamas to negotiate any meaningful resolution of disputes and hope for peace in the Middle East and beyond. And people of good will must do all within their power to bring a united, strong, independent, secure and prosperous Palestine into existence now.

– *Ramsey Clark, January. 15, 2011*

I

Hamas Sweeps the 2006 Palestinian Elections

"I would say the three most perfect elections that we have monitored have been in Palestine."
—Jimmy Carter, as reported by National Public Radio.
Former U.S. President Carter is founder of the Carter Center, which has observed 81 elections in 33 countries.

The Palestinian Authority elections have been among the most heavily monitored ever by international observers. For example, the European Union supplied election observers to assess the whole Palestinian election process, including the legal framework for those voting in the Israeli-occupied territories of the West Bank, Gaza and East Jerusalem.

In the first PA election in 1996, Fatah head Yasser Arafat was voted in as president. After Arafat's death, Fatah candidate Mahmoud Abbas, who was heavily favored by Washington, was elected to replace him as president on Jan. 9, 2005. Fatah, the largest of the Palestinian groups, has long dominated Palestinian politics and many on the international arena, including in the U.S. government, expected this to continue.

December 15, 2005, marked the last of a yearlong series of local council elections in the West Bank and Gaza. When the ballots in that election were counted and all the municipal results weighed, the Islamic Resistance

Movement, or Hamas, had won 73 percent of the vote, giving this group control of 13 of the 15 Palestinian municipalities. Israel and Western governments, especially the U.S., had not expected such an outcome.

A month later, on Jan. 25, 2006, elections were held for the Legislative Council, the legislature of the PA. The Bush administration had heavily pushed the Palestinian elections, especially of the legislature, claiming these elections were "bringing Western democracy" to the Palestinian people. The Bush administration and the regime in Israel believed that the Fatah leadership, which already held the presidency, would be victorious.

When all the votes were counted, however, Hamas swept the election, winning 74 seats to Fatah's 45 seats. Hamas won most of the 132 seats and could form a majority government of the Palestine National Authority on its own.

It was incontestable that the Palestinian people had voted their choice, as they had been observed doing so by scores of international election monitors. The turnout was a very high 74 percent, according to the PA's Central Elections Commission. The small army of international observers present declared the elections free and fair, even exemplary.

However, for Washington, Tel Aviv and most governments in Europe, the results were a bombshell. The Palestinian people had chosen the "wrong" group to represent them. These powers responded by trying to envenom relations between Fatah and Hamas. Israel's response was to punish the Palestinian people for their election choice by increasing military incursions into the West Bank and Gaza, kidnapping and arresting elected Hamas officials, and trying to assassinate the prime minister of the PA, a member of Hamas.

Palestinian vote jolts the imperialists

By Michael Kramer
Published Jan. 31, 2006

For the second time in a six-week period, Palestinians have voted in elections that they have run themselves. The results were not what the Bush administration had expected or had wanted them to be.

Municipal elections were conducted in the West Bank on Dec. 15, 2005. On Jan. 25, 2006, elections for the Palestinian Legislative Council were held in the West Bank, Gaza and East Jerusalem.

The elections were conducted much more fairly and efficiently than those held in Florida and Ohio during the U.S. presidential elections of

2000 and 2004. In the U.S., millions of African Americans, Latinos/as, immigrants, youth and a transient working class face a gauntlet of local, state and federal laws regarding residency and past experiences with the police, courts and jails that effectively prohibit them from voting.

Palestinians in Israel and diaspora denied right to vote

In Palestine, only Palestinians living in the West Bank, Gaza and East Jerusalem—areas occupied in June 1967 by the U.S.-armed and U.S.-financed Zionist military—were allowed to vote. Millions of Palestinians living in areas of Palestine occupied in 1948; in refugee camps in Lebanon, Syria and Jordan; and in a diaspora that stretches from Paterson, N.J., to Sydney, Australia, were denied the right to vote through a combination of apartheid-like Zionist election laws and the 1993 U.S.-sponsored Oslo Accords.

Washington favored Fatah

The U.S. favored the Palestinian National Liberation Movement, or Fatah, in both elections. Fatah was given millions of dollars, both above ground and under the table, to help fund its campaign. While many in its leadership have been cultivated by the U.S. since the early 1990s and have overtly cooperated with the Pentagon and CIA, rank-and-file Fatah members—especially youth—have been militant, heroic and self-sacrificing in confronting the Zionist occupation since the resistance group's first military operation on Jan. 3, 1965.

The organization has recently split into at least two factions and is in the midst of a serious internal crisis. Marwan Barghouti is the most popular and charismatic leader of Fatah. He has been imprisoned by the Zionists since April 2002.

The people chose Hamas

The big winner in the PA cabinet and legislature elections was the Islamic Resistance Movement, or Hamas. Hamas was organized in 1987 by a current in Palestinian society based in the religious community that was not comfortable working in secular political organizations. This group has always shown a willingness to adapt to changing circumstances, however.

In the past Hamas refused to take part in any Palestinian election because of the elections' association with Annex 1 of the Oslo Accords. The 1993 Oslo Accords, signed by the Palestinian leaders, explicitly recognized Israel and limited their demands to the creation of a Palestinian state only in the West Bank and Gaza, 22 percent of historic Palestine. Hamas does not recognize Israel, and asserts the right of Palestinians to return to all historic Palestine.

Support for the Zionist occupation of Palestine has been a fundamental tenet of the U.S. government since the 1930s. Like the resistance in Iraq, the victory of Hamas calls into question the future of U.S. imperialism and its allies in the region.

Why did Hamas win?

Hamas won because Palestinian voters were fed up with the rampant corruption and disorganization of the Fatah-led government of the recent period. Fifteen years of Fatah-led negotiations and compromises with the Zionists had not produced any improvement in daily Palestinian life.

Thousands of Palestinians are jailed. Precious land continues to be ruined or confiscated and turned over to Zionist settlers, many of whom are new arrivals from the U.S. and Russia. The apartheid wall that cuts through Palestinian West Bank towns insults the senses of all who love Palestine.

Hamas has a high level of organizational ability and has established an extensive social service network in Gaza. It distributes material, educational and medical aid with great efficiency. This is what the population demands.

Washington responds to vote with threats

Hours after the election results were announced, the Bush administration began demanding that Hamas recognize the Israeli settler state and end armed resistance to occupation or else face a cutoff of all aid from the U.S. and the European Union. Hamas has refused these demands. When has Israel ever recognized the national rights of the Palestinians?

At this time, it is most important for all those active in the Palestine solidarity movement, as well as anti-Zionists and peace activists, to maintain and continue their work. U.S. imperialism will try its best to encourage civil war in Palestine. Its allies are already trying to divide the solidarity and peace movements by raising certain contradictions in the religious-based social program of Hamas, as well as historical inaccuracies in its charter.

Imperialism must not be allowed to succeed.

Let's you and him fight

U.S., Israel, European governments try to
increase Fatah-Hamas tensions

Editorial
Published Jan. 10, 2007

The U.S., France and other imperialist powers claim to be "appalled" over fighting between the Palestinian groups Fatah and Hamas. U.S. Secretary of State Condoleezza Rice's recent call for a halt to the fighting, however, is sheer hypocrisy. Washington, Tel Aviv and the European powers have used every weapon in their arsenal to exacerbate tensions between Fatah and Hamas.

In January 2006, the Palestinian people overwhelmingly voted in legislative elections for Hamas, a group known for determined struggle against occupation. Neither U.S. finance capital nor its clients in Tel Aviv accepted the Palestinian people's choice and have waged a most brutal campaign for "regime change" ever since.

A year of economic warfare on PA

For the last year, Israel, the U.S. and European regimes have waged economic war on the Palestinian Authority to render it ineffective. The U.S. and Europe have withheld promised funds, and U.S. banks have imposed a financial blockade on PA banks, denying the PA funds from Arab League countries or anyone else. Israel has held back the $55 million in PA tax monies it collects monthly. These funds account for a third of the PA's budget and pay the wages of the PA's 160,000 civil servants, including the security forces involved in current clashes. A third of the Palestinian population depends on this money to survive.

Every day Israel attacks, bombards and arrests

At the same time, Israeli occupation forces—bankrolled and armed by the U.S.—have laid siege to Gaza and the West Bank, continue daily military incursions, bombings, arrests, huge land confiscations and destruction of homes, and are building the apartheid wall. Some call these assaults the most serious in the entire history of the Palestinian struggle.

It is within the context of this brutal economic squeeze, military onslaught and truly untenable situation for the Palestinian people that tensions have risen between Fatah and Hamas.

Weapon of 'divide and conquer'

Imperialism is trying to use the weapon of "divide and conquer" to disrupt the struggle in Palestine, just as it is used to "Balkanize" Iraq. Washington and Tel Aviv now clearly favor Mahmoud Abbas of Fatah, who is the PA president, over Hamas, which controls the PA cabinet and legislature. Before Hamas became part of the PA government, however, Israel vilified Abbas and refused to speak with him.

In the name of "peace," the U.S. and Israel are waging war against the PA and the people who have elected Hamas. But the real goal is to destroy every attempt by the Palestinian people to assert true self-determination and build a sovereign Palestine. Palestinian sovereignty provides the only hope for true peace.

Without interference, Palestinians can resolve differences

This is one of the most difficult times in the history of the Palestinian resistance. International support is needed more than ever to lift the siege on the heroic Palestinian national liberation struggle. The anti-war movement here in the U.S. can be most helpful by renewing the fighting to get U.S. imperialism out of the Middle East, and to stop all U.S. aid to Israel.

Free from the bone-crushing burden of foreign interference and U.S.-financed Israeli domination, the Palestinian people can and will resolve peacefully any differences among them on how to best liberate and run their country.

Facts on the ground

Tel Aviv attacked the Palestinian Authority and people long before Hamas won the elections

By Joyce Chediac
Published April 27, 2006

The Israeli government claims that its recent attacks on the Palestinian Authority stem from Hamas's electoral win. However, a look at Israeli actions in the last few years shows that Tel Aviv disregarded the PA and attacked the Palestinian people and infrastructure long before Hamas was an electoral majority in the PA. Here are some statistics on Israeli attacks on Palestinians from September 2000 to March 2004, gathered by the *Palestine Monitor*, an independent Palestinian publication based in Ramallah, the occupied West Bank.

Deaths and injuries: 2,859 Palestinians killed, 19 percent of them children; more than 41,000 injured and 2,500 permanently disabled.

Attacks on medical personnel and services: 25 medical personnel were killed while on duty, 425 injured and 121 ambulances attacked and damaged. Palestine Medical Committee ambulances were denied access at roadblocks 991 times. According to the Palestinian Ministry of Health, 129 sick Palestinians actually died at roadblocks, denied access to treatment. Hospitals and clinics were attacked and damaged 291 times and 71 emergency personnel and volunteers arrested.

Checkpoints: 120 Israeli checkpoints in the West Bank and Gaza divide the West Bank into 300 separate clusters and the Gaza Strip into three separate clusters. The West Bank was held under severe internal closure 66 percent of the days, and partial internal closure 34 percent of the days; Gaza 94 percent of the days. Closure causes water and gas shortages and other humanitarian problems.

Arrests and detentions: From March 2002 to March 2004, 15,000 Palestinians have been detained, 6,000 of whom remain imprisoned; 1,700 have neither been tried nor had charges brought against them.

Some 350 Palestinian children are incarcerated, 30 without being charged. Many of the prisoners are subjected to torture and don't receive adequate medical attention.

Property damage: More than $666 million in Palestinian residential property was destroyed or looted; 720 homes destroyed by selling and demolition, and 11,553 damaged, affecting 73,600 people; 34,606 olive and fruit trees were uprooted, 1,162.4 dunums (287 acres) of land confiscated and 14,339 dunums (3,558 acres) of land bulldozed or burned.

Economic conditions: Total Palestinian income losses were estimated at between $3.2 billion to $10 billion. This does not include the cost of the destruction of public and private property. Total income lost in wages was $59.4 million. Unemployment in Gaza was 67 percent, in the West Bank 48 percent. Israel prevented 125,000 Palestinians from going to work.

The wall: The border between Israel and the West Bank is 230 miles, but the 15-foot concrete wall now being built will be double that length, snaking through the West Bank, separating and strangling Palestinian communities. United Nations Office for the Coordination of Human Affairs Director David Shearer said the establishment of the wall has led to the confiscation of 35,000 dunums (8,469 acres) of West Bank land so far.

'Democratic' Israel tries to wipe out elected Palestinians

Prime minister's office bombed, 64 officials kidnapped

By Deirdre Griswold
Published July 5, 2006

Every self-righteous excuse for the U.S. bankrolling of Israel's endless aggressions against the Arab and Muslim people was shredded this week—and not for the first time.

Think of the claim that Israel represents the only true "democracy" in the Middle East. Yet here were Israeli tanks and planes attacking the Palestinian Authority in Gaza, sending missiles into the office of the prime minister (fortunately, he wasn't there) and arresting most of the top government officials.

New York protest June 30, 2006, hits Israel's assault on Gaza.

WW photo: Deirdre Griswold

Nobody disputed election results

Yes, elected officials. The Palestinian people went to the polls in January and chose the party they wanted to represent them. Nobody disputed the results of the election, which Hamas won. Wasn't that a triumph for democracy? Especially since the people voted for the party that promised to fight hardest to defend their national identity and regain the lands that Israel took from them. That was a difficult thing to do, since they knew Israel, with the U.S. behind it, would find a way to strike back.

And it has. Israeli tanks swept into Gaza on June 28, 2006. Its fighter planes have been pounding away at power plants, the water supply and other essential elements of the infrastructure, leading to a major humanitarian crisis. Some 750,000 people in Gaza now have no electricity and no running water—during the hottest part of the year. It is a wonder that they survive.

Israel's commandos have gone after the very people the Palestinians elected to represent them. To be precise, they have kidnapped 64 Palestinian governmental ministers and politicians since Israel began its assault on Gaza. Israeli planes also bombed the home of Palestinian Prime Minister Ismael Haniyeh.

All this is supposed to be in retaliation for the capture of one Israeli soldier, Gilad Shalit. But in the weeks before that happened, the Israeli military had killed more than 30 Palestinian civilians, including three children and a pregnant woman.

Israeli raid attempt to derail Hamas-Fatah agreement

There is speculation that Israel was trying to provoke a response in order to derail an agreement just concluded between the two major Palestinian parties, Hamas and Fatah, that could move forward negotiations for a peace settlement with Israel. Certainly, the Israeli people want peace, too—but their government is doing everything it can to keep such a thing from happening.

Israeli commentator calls Tel Aviv 'terror' state

Even inside Israel, the government's assault is being heavily criticized. Commentator Gideon Levy of the newspaper *Ha'aretz* wrote, "A state that takes such steps is no longer distinguishable from a terror organization."

Who really keeps this horrible war and occupation going? The answer is not just Tel Aviv but also the U.S. government, which has built Israel into a military fortress to protect imperialist interests in the Middle East, especially the overweening lust of U.S. big business for the fabulous profits to be made from oil.

Washington gives Israel $3 billion a year in weapons

The U.S. government spends $3 billion a year in military aid on this small country—which comes to more than $8.5 million each day just for arms. When all U.S. aid to Israel is totaled, it comes to $15 million a day (*Washington Report on Middle East Affairs*, September 2003). Of course, that money comes from U.S. taxpayers. On the other hand, the profits from selling military equipment and oil products don't go to the U.S. people—they go to the big corporations that find ways to pay practically nothing in taxes. So war or peace, it's a win-win situation for the super-rich.

WW II record shows U.S. let Jewish people die

Instead of rescuing Jewish people from Nazi-occupied Europe during the Holocaust, Washington's policy was to wait instead until after the war and then throw them into Palestine, where they were told by the Zionist political movement that no one lived there anyway. The growth of this racist, settler state, which fought several wars with neighboring countries to expand its territory and treats the indigenous Palestinians as less than human, has only inflamed the whole area.

For centuries Jews and Muslims lived together peacefully

Throughout the Middle East, where for centuries Jews and Muslims lived amicably side by side, there is now the deepest animosity because of Israel's aggressions.

What the U.S. government is doing to the Palestinians is illegal. Under the U.S. Arms Export Control Act of 1976, military hardware sold by the United States can only be used for defensive purposes or to maintain internal security. Nevertheless, Israel has used U.S.-supplied F-16 fighter jets, "Apache" and Cobra attack helicopters, 15mm howitzers, M-16 automatic rifles, M50 machine guns and many other weapons and ammunition to attack Palestinian towns and cities.

There is growing sentiment inside the U.S., expressed especially in progressive youth culture, to support the Palestinian cause and stop the bankrolling of Israel. It's an issue that should be taken up in every union, every community organization, and every school.

II

Hamas Assumes Control of Gaza

"Our fight is not against Fatah ... but against just one group of Fatah agents who were following the Zionist agenda."
— Abu Obaida, spokesperson for Hamas's Qassam Brigades
   (*Observer,* June 17, 2007)

In mid-June 2007, Hamas staged a military operation against Fatah in Gaza and seized control, ousting Fatah from all Gaza government positions. The international media raised a hysteria against Hamas, branding it the "aggressor" in a "power struggle between factions." This chapter takes a closer look at these events and finds that Hamas was not the aggressor, nor was this a power struggle between factions. Hamas's military move was a reactive one meant to pre-empt a coup attempt by a small group armed and trained by the Bush administration and following a U.S. plan. Washington, Tel Aviv and the European powers were caught unaware by Hamas's action.

The sequence of events reported here was pieced together from many different media sources while the news was breaking. Ten months later, the events and analysis reported here were documented from primary sources— confidential U.S. government documents and interviews with U.S. officials— made available to journalist David Rose and used by him in his article, "The Gaza Bombshell," in the April 2008 issue of Vanity Fair. The blurb for that article reads:

"After failing to anticipate Hamas's victory over Fatah in the 2006 Palestinian election, the White House cooked up yet another scandalously covert and self-defeating Middle East debacle: part Iran-contra, part Bay of Pigs. With confidential documents, corroborated by outraged former and current U.S. officials, the author reveals how President [George W.] Bush, Condoleezza Rice, and Deputy National Security Adviser Elliott Abrams backed an armed force under Fatah strongman Muhammad Dahlan, touching off a bloody civil war in Gaza, leaving Hamas stronger than ever."

Chronology:

How the U.S. plotted for 18 months to overthrow the unity government and remove Hamas

By Joyce Chediac
Published June 24, 2007

In mid-June 2007, Hamas staged a pre-emptive coup against elements in Fatah and, after three days of fighting, took control of Gaza, with Fatah losing all governing power there.

The U.S., Israeli and European governments, and the establishment media in these countries, have heaped all blame on Hamas for this move. Not talked about is the fact that the Abbas-Dahlan clique within

Fatah had allowed itself to be the agent of a U.S.-Israeli planned coup against Hamas, designed to topple the unity government. Hamas's military moves in Gaza this month were defensive actions to prevent that coup.

Here's how it went:

January 2006: To the shock of Tel Aviv and Washington, close to 80 percent of the Palestinian electorate vote for Hamas, giving it a substantial majority in the Palestinian Authority's Legislative Council.

February 2006: A program attributed to U.S. Deputy National Security Advisor Elliott Abrams calls for giving Fatah guns, ammunition and training, and getting them to fight Hamas for control of the Palestinian government. Abrams is known for getting funds to Nicaraguan contras in the 1980s and covering up massacres and atrocities committed against civilians in El Salvador by U.S.-backed militias and death squads. (*Asia Times*, May 16, 2007; Conflicts Forum, Jan. 7, 2007; electronicintifada.net, June 14, 2007)

January 2007: The Bush administration announces plans to give $86 million to "fortify Mr. Abbas against armed assaults from Hamas." The security program "reflects the basic sense in the administration that the only way to change things is through confrontation." (*Wall Street Journal,* Jan. 12, 2007)

Much of these funds were earmarked for "unaccountable militias, particularly the 'Preventive Security Force' headed by Gaza warlord Mohammad Dahlan, a close ally of Israel and the United States, and the Abbas-affiliated 'Presidential Guard.'" (electronicintifada.net, June 14, 2007) Peter Beaumont, foreign affairs editor of the British *Observer*, called Dahlan "the man widely credited with beginning the cycle of violence in Gaza." (June 17, 2007)

February 2007: Hamas and Fatah, in an agreement brokered in Mecca by Saudi Arabia, form a national unity government that will place their militias under the control of a neutral interior minister. However, Abbas and Dahlan refuse to honor this agreement and continue to amass weapons. (Conflicts Forum, Jan. 7, 2007)

At that time, a senior Hamas official said of Dahlan, "This man has been involved in the American-backed plot to topple our government." (*Jerusalem Post*, Feb. 14, 2007)

In addition to supplying guns, ammunition and training to Fatah forces to take on Hamas in the streets of Gaza and the West Bank, by this time the U.S. government had arranged for the training of a large number of Fatah military personnel at camps in Ramallah and Jericho in the Israeli-occupied West Bank.

May 2007: "Israel this week allowed the Palestinian party Fatah to bring into the Gaza Strip as many as 500 fresh troops trained under a U.S.-coordinated program to counter Hamas. ... The troops were trained by Egyptian authorities under a program coordinated by Lt. Gen. Keith W. Dayton, a special U.S. envoy to the region." Additionally, the U.S. government "approved $40 million to train the Palestinian Presidential Guard, a force of about 4,000 troops. ... Although it is under Abbas' authority, the Presidential Guard is run by Mohammed Dahlan." (*Washington Post*, May 18, 2007)

Israeli paper of record *Ha'aretz* publishes on May 4, 2007, the full text of another U.S. plan, "Benchmarks for Agreement on Movement and Access," which details deadlines for Israeli dismantling of roadblocks, with Mohammad Dahlan drawing up and implementing a security plan to stop Qassam rocket fire into Israel—code words for suppressing Hamas. The forces under Dahlan must be deployed to "problem areas no later than [the] date" of June 21. (*Asia Times*, May 16, 2007)

June 2007: With this plan and date as a backdrop, senior Fatah officials in the Gaza Strip ask Israel "to allow them to receive large shipments of arms and ammunition from Arab countries, including Egypt." This includes "armored cars, hundreds of armor-piercing RPG rockets, thousands of hand grenades and millions of rounds of ammunition for small caliber weapons." (*Ha'aretz*, June 7, 2007)

Laila el-Haddad, a writer for Aljazeera.net, said that while waiting to pass through the Rafah crossing from Gaza into Egypt on June 7 she saw "several hundred" Palestinian troops enter Gaza. (democracynow.org, June 15, 2007) This appears to have been part of Fatah's strike force.

In a preemptive move, in mid-June Hamas took control of Fatah's national police headquarters, the border crossing with Egypt, the Preventive Security headquarters, Fatah's intelligence services, the Presidential Guard offices and media. While Fatah forces were more numerous and better armed, they were demoralized and offered little resistance.

National resistance confronts imperialism in Palestine

By Joyce Chediac
Published June 24, 2007

Recent events in Gaza were not a "power struggle between rival factions" or a "five-day civil war." These descriptions in the establishment press are attempts to conceal the events' true nature.

The Gaza struggle was between irreconcilable class forces. On one side were the forces of national resistance represented by Hamas. On the other side were the forces of imperialist slavery represented by a small faction of Fatah under Palestinian President Mahmoud Abbas and his security advisor, Mohammad Dahlan. This group consciously lent itself to the designs of Washington and Tel Aviv to drive Hamas from power and overturn the results of the 2006 election that gave Hamas a majority in the Palestinian Legislative Council.

"Our fight is not against Fatah, the one with the long history in the struggle, but against just one group of Fatah agents who were following the Zionist agenda," explained Abu Obaida, spokesperson for Hamas's Qassam Brigades. (*Observer*, June 17, 2007) Hamas recognizes Mahmoud Abbas, and has called on him to join them in a new unity government.

Hamas moved in self-defense

Hamas was compelled to defend itself by destroying the armed forces of the cat's-paw of colonialism before this cat's-paw destroyed Hamas. This is why Hamas staged a pre-emptive assault on Fatah security offices, especially the Preventive Security forces and the Presidential Guard, which reported to Mohammad Dahlan. In the heat of events, genuinely anti-imperialist, anti-Zionist militants in Fatah may have erroneously been drawn into the struggle against Hamas. This, however, does not change the struggle's class character.

The U.S., Israel, the Arab League and European Union have quickly lined up against Hamas, issuing further threats to that group and to the 1.5 million people of Gaza. Hamas and the Palestinian struggle need the support of progressives worldwide at this crucial time.

Group tried to assassinate Hamas prime minister

Palestinians, so much in need of a strong and united movement, have reacted to the Gaza developments and ensuing split with a heavy heart. Under constant attack by Israel, the situation in the Occupied Territories is dire. But it would have been worse if Hamas had been defeated in Gaza by the Fatah group. This group countered every attempt by Hamas to achieve unity against the Israelis and stood by while Israel arrested 64 Hamas legislators and other officials. The group persisted in provocation, even to the point of trying to assassinate Hamas Prime Minister Ismail Haniyeh.

At U.S. insistence, Abbas dissolves elected unity government

Continuing its blatant intervention, "The United States had quietly encouraged Mr. Abbas to dissolve the Palestinian government and dismiss Prime Minister Ismail Haniyeh." (*New York Times*, June 15, 2007) This is exactly what Abbas did, ignoring offers from Hamas to re-establish the unity government.

In violation of the Palestinian Constitution, and much to the joy of Washington, Abbas has fired Hamas and the entire elected government, appointed an emergency government and appointed as prime minister Salam Fayyad, a former World Bank official who is the West's economic point man. This new government, in which only Abbas was elected, claims to preside over the West Bank but really rules by the iron fist of Israeli occupation, where all the struggle forces must remain underground.

Now Bush is calling Abbas "president of all the Palestinians," and Israeli Prime Minister Ehud Olmert is calling Abbas "friend." However, neither Washington nor Tel Aviv has any intention of granting true sovereignty to the Palestinian people, out of fear of their revolutionary potential.

U.S. and Israel caught unawares

The fall of the Fatah security forces caught U.S. and Israel unawares and dealt them a stunning defeat. Even a *New York Times* editorial calls events in Gaza "a defeat for Israeli and American policy." (June 15,

2007) The U.S., which looks upon the people as commodities to be bought and sold, was truly shocked at how quickly the more numerous and better-armed Fatah forces collapsed before Hamas.

However, people are not commodities. They have hearts and minds. Though poverty may have driven many into the security forces, many Fatah soldiers had no heart for enforcing a pro-Zionist, pro-imperialist agenda on their own people.

The *Observer* (June 17, 2007) reports that people within Fatah support the Hamas move. According to the *Observer*, Hamas "produced a former senior Fatah member—Khaled Abu Helah—on its TV station to say that he welcomed Hamas's cleansing of Fatah of its collaborators and traitors."

A witness told the *Observer*, "Some officers in the [Fatah] Presidential Guard had sent their men home as the fighting began."

Another Gaza resident told the *Observer*, "Hamas fighters were not getting salaries. They believed in what they were doing. Some fought for four days without going home."

Fatah forces did not defend their stations, 'Won't fight for an American agenda'

This Gazan continued, "Fatah security forces fought for their thousand shekels or a pack of cigarettes. Dahlan had used poverty to recruit the people. The majority didn't even turn up to defend their stations. Many stayed home. Most were in plain clothes. Dozens called the Qassam [Hamas] and said, 'We want to leave, give us security and a safe passage.' Most of the decent security people don't want to fight for Dahlan, or Israel or America. They don't feel they should be killed for the American or Israeli agenda."

There were earlier times when Fatah forces felt they had something to fight for. One of their finest moments occurred during the 1982 U.S.-Israeli siege of Beirut. For seven weeks, Israel attacked Beirut by sea, air and land, cutting off food and water supplies and disconnecting the electricity in blistering heat. However, the armed people and heroic fighters, who mostly identified with Fatah, held strong under the most unbearable conditions, defended the camps and suburbs, and would not give in. Their steadfastness forced a negotiated settlement and inspired workers and oppressed people everywhere.

These Fatah fighters showed the world that only the struggle wins concessions, especially in a national liberation struggle as beleaguered as the fight for Palestine. Today Hamas is the group most under attack for waging this struggle. It, and all who fight for Palestine, sorely need the active support of all who value justice and freedom.

New Palestinian premier
has U.S. 'blessing'

Published June 24, 2007

Salam Fayyad, whom Mahmoud Abbas unilaterally named premier in a government meant to bypass Hamas, was appointed "with the explicit blessing of the U.S.," said Peter Beaumont, foreign affairs editor of the *Observer*. (June 17, 2007) Fayyad has no known credentials in the struggle to liberate Palestine.

Before the appointment, this former World Bank official was "trying to drum up support to have international aid sent through a special Palestine Liberation Organization bank account in order to avoid Hamas." (*New York Times*, June 16, 2007)

"In last year's elections to the Palestinian Legislative Council—the election Hamas won—Fayyad's list secured just 2.4 percent of votes." Beaumont continued. "He is largely unknown to most Palestinians. He has no party machinery to support him.

"The only people who are really behind Salam Fayyad are the European and U.S. diplomats who have long sung his praises behind the scenes to any journalist prepared to listen."

Hamas: 'We were forced to do it'

By Joyce Chediac
Published June 24, 2007

The worldwide imperialist establishment and its media blame Hamas for staging a coup against the Palestinian unity government in Gaza. For a more accurate picture, a statement from Hamas follows, excerpted from www.Manartv.com.lb (June 16, 2007).

"Hamas does not want to seize power," said the group's politburo chief Khaled Mershaal. "We are faithful to the Palestinian people."

Mershaal added, "What has happened in Gaza is an emergency measure to deal with a state that wanted to impose itself on everybody. ... [W]e were forced to take this emergency measure. We did not want to take it but we were forced to do it. ... We want brotherhood with the sons of the Fatah movement. This was not a confrontation with Fatah. Our crisis is not with Fatah."

"The people [of Gaza] were suffering from chaos and lack of security and this treatment was needed," Mershaal continued. "The lack of security drove the crisis toward explosion. ... "

"Abbas has legitimacy," Mershaal said. "There's no one who would question or doubt that he is an elected president, and we will cooperate with him for the sake of national interest."

Mershaal called upon Arab League foreign ministers meeting in Cairo to help mediate talks between Hamas and Abbas, to act "as an umbrella to hold the national Palestinian dialogue to approach a Palestinian accord."

Mershaal said that a national unity government is the only solution, and that Abbas' dissolution of the unity government "will not remedy the situation ... and will not solve the problem. There will be no two governments and no division of the homeland."

Meanwhile, Hamas official Sami Abu Zuhri said, "The appointment of Salam Fayyad as a head of the emergency government is a coup against [Hamas's] legitimacy. ... We ask President Abbas to withdraw the decision in order to preserve the integrity of our people."

III

Isolated by land, sea and air blockade –
Israel Turns Gaza into
a New Warsaw Ghetto

In March 2006, the U.S., Israel and the European Union began a boycott of the new Hamas government in Gaza, punishing the civilian population by suspending all economic ties, curtailing U.N. refugee aid, shutting down charities, and even withholding the Palestinians' own tax money. After Hamas ousted Fatah from the Gaza government in June 2007, these same forces tightened this boycott into an all-out land, sea and air blockade, besieging the people of Gaza.

Collective punishment is a war crime

U.S.- backed siege tries to break people's spirit through starvation

Editorial published Sept. 27, 2007

Since the Israeli settler state seized the West Bank and Gaza Strip in 1967, it has treated the two territories populated by Palestinians in the tradition of a colonial power. It imposes Israeli rules, treats the residents as if they have no rights, reacts with violence against those who resist being a colonized people, arrests thousands indiscriminately and jails without trial other thousands. It murders scores of leaders with "targeted assassinations."

Tel Aviv has broken all its interim agreements with the Palestinians. It has erected a wall that runs through the West Bank and divides Palestinian villages; disguised as security, this wall has been used to seize another piece of that already small territory.

Now, the Israeli state has imposed a siege on Gaza and declared Gaza an "enemy entity," restricting even humanitarian aid.

Israel made this new definition at the same time Secretary of State Condoleezza Rice was visiting the Middle East with the alleged objective of organizing an "International Conference of Peace." Rice raised no objections; she even echoed the Israeli definition of Gaza as an "enemy entity." She called Hamas, the party the Palestinians elected to head their government, a "terrorist organization."

Clearly, Rice's visit had little to do with "peace," as she claims. Her visit is part of U.S. plans to reorganize that part of the world to serve the interests of U.S. monopoly capital. Washington and Wall Street rely on Israel as an adjunct military force in the region that has always sided with the imperialists against the efforts of Arab and other Muslim peoples to liberate their national territory and resources, especially the oil, from nearly a century of Western domination.

This U.S.-Israeli attempt to define 1.5 million Palestinians in Gaza as "enemies" is collective punishment, which was condemned in world forums when the Nazi imperialists did it. It can only increase the suffering of the Palestinian people of Gaza.

This is also part of the U.S.-European Union-Israeli strategy to divide the Palestinian people. The tactic is to promote Fatah, which not too long ago was itself being assailed by Washington as "terrorist," against Hamas, while trying to break the people's spirit through starvation.

Conditions grow desperate as food, fuel, medicine, water denied

Yet resistance continues

By Sara Flounders
Published Jan. 5, 2008

Israeli Prime Minister Ehud Olmert had rejected overtures by Hamas for discussions about even a temporary cease-fire. (*New York Times*, Dec. 24, 2007)

Now there are increasing calls within Israel, including from the head of the Israeli military, for a full-scale invasion of besieged and isolated Gaza.

Death and sickness increasing

Conditions today in Gaza are desperate; Israel severely restricts and in some cases even denies the entrance of even basic food, fuel and electricity. Water filters, water pumps and bottled water are barred. The most basic supplies, from soap to batteries for hearing aids, are prohibited. No spare parts of any kind are permitted. Even desperately needed incubators for babies or dialysis equipment cannot be repaired or replaced.

In the cold and crowded wards of Gaza City's Shifa Hospital, the dispensary is out of 85 essential medicines and is close to using up almost 150 others.

There are rolling blackouts across the Strip. Previously Gaza barely functioned on 80,000 gallons of diesel fuel a day. Now Israel has reduced this to less than a third. Less than 24,000 gallons of diesel fuel a day are allowed in.

Without fuel and functioning pumps, Gaza cannot even dispose of its sewage. This has become a major sanitation threat. Piles of garbage rot in the streets and in vacant lots due to the shortages of fuel to operate garbage trucks.

Rising inflation but no jobs

Practically all businesses are closed and their workers laid off for lack of raw materials. With all supplies severely restricted, inflation is spiraling to five and 10 times the prices of a year ago.

Travel into and out of Gaza is banned. Even severely sick patients cannot leave Gaza for treatment in hospitals in Israel, Egypt, Jordan or any other country. Health clinics, lacking supplies, are shutting down.

Previously 900 trucks a day entered Gaza carrying supplies. Now Israel has reduced the number to 15 trucks a day. A short list of about half a dozen basic articles is allowed in.

Gaza is a mere 25 miles long and only 6 miles wide. It is one of the poorest and most densely populated areas of the world. Most of the population is refugees who were expelled from their land by Zionist forces. They are destitute and have relied for decades on U.N. relief supplies and remittances from Palestinians working abroad for the most basic necessities. Now even these sources are being choked off.

However, Gaza has always been a center of resistance to the Zionist state. Both the first Palestinian Intifada, or uprising, 20 years ago and the Intifada that started in 2000 began in Gaza.

Because of the unrelenting Palestinian struggle against Zionist settlers, in 2005 Israel was forced to withdraw from Gaza 8,000 of its colonizers, who had for 37 years seized the best land and available water for themselves.

But after withdrawing the settlers, Israel refused to allow a Palestinian state of any kind to function. Gaza, with a population of 1.5 million people, was turned into a rigidly controlled concentration camp.

Gaza isolated in land, sea and air blockade

Israel destroyed the airport and blocked the building of a harbor. All connections with the outside world were cut; even the sea lanes and fishing boats were blocked. The long-promised "safe passage" road between the Gaza Strip and the West Bank was sealed. All crossings in and out of the Strip are under total Israeli control.

Previously, tens of thousands of workers from Gaza had to cross into Israel to work as low-paid day laborers. Now even this bare-survival employment is terminated.

The resistance has the people's support

Despite desperate conditions of siege and almost total blockade, resistance continues.

Maintaining resistance in the face of the onerous siege has the overwhelming support of the population. The Palestinian resistance lacks jet aircraft, helicopters, radar, anti-aircraft batteries, tanks, electronic surveillance, satellite reconnaissance or any of the other sophisticated high-tech equipment that the Pentagon has endlessly supplied to Israel.

Yet not a day passes that Qassam rocket barrages are not fired at Israel. These rockets and grenades are machine-tooled by hand in garages or smuggled in. The southern Israeli town of Sderot is the closest target, but rockets are fired all along the borders of Gaza. For months, more than 10 rockets or mortars have been fired from Gaza each day.

Despite the totally unequal struggle and the conditions of almost total deprivation, resistance fighters in Gaza have managed to accumulate primitive weapons and basic explosives. They are smuggled into the Strip through the many tunnels under its border with Egypt. The endless digging of miles of tunnels is itself an enormous accomplishment.

Israel's high-tech army kills at will in Gaza and West Bank

The unequal and overwhelming Israeli force versus the fierce Palestinian resistance can be seen in just one week of attacks.

According to the Palestinian Web news service Electronic Intifada, on Dec. 20, 2007, on the eve of the celebration of the Muslim holiday Eid al-Adha, a special Israeli unit sneaked into the Palestinian village of al-Msadar in the middle area of Gaza from the eastern border fence. Once there, Israeli soldiers stormed six tall buildings and held their inhabitants. They set up sniper nests. By early morning, an Israeli Occupation Forces unit, reinforced by four armored bulldozers and 10 tanks, took positions in the area. Meanwhile, the Israeli Defense Forces launched air strikes and artillery attacks, killing both civilians and fighters who responded to the attack.

Two days earlier an IDF spy drone had fired two missiles into one of the most densely populated areas in Gaza, killing four people whom Israel claimed were militants, near the at-Touba mosque in Jabaliya refugee camp

On the same day, an IDF fighter jet fired a missile that hit a car on Said Aal-Aas street in the al-Nasir neighborhood of Gaza City. Two people in the car were killed.

A day earlier, on Dec. 17, 2007, the IDF fired two ground-to-ground missiles at four people in a field located in the al-Zaytoun neighborhood in the south of Gaza City. The four were killed.

In the West Bank, Israeli forces also continue to stage attacks, kidnappings and missile strikes. The entire West Bank, the other small fragment of Palestinian land occupied by Israel since 1967, has been carved into numerous tiny pieces, surrounded by walls and hundreds of IDF police checkpoints.

Full invasion of Gaza threatened

IDF Chief of Staff Gabi Ashkenazi declared in mid-December 2007 that the Israeli Army should enter the Gaza Strip in a large-scale military operation.

In past decades, Israeli forces have invaded Gaza many times at a cost of thousands of Palestinian lives and massive destruction in efforts to smash the resistance. However, what is now causing apprehension and great concern in Israel is that its forces will pay a price. In the past year Palestinian mines, and possibly anti-tank missiles, have been able to penetrate Israeli's heavily armored 60-ton Merkava Mark-3 tanks. On Dec. 12, 2007, an Israeli tank was hit while on a raid inside Gaza.

Out of fear that Hamas forces in Gaza might have obtained anti-aircraft missiles, the Israeli Air Force now uses only helicopters equipped with anti-missile defenses when flying over the Strip.

The problem for U.S. and Zionist forces is that they have been unable to defeat the will and determination of the Palestinian people to fight for full self-determination and the right of all Palestinian people to return to their land.

Mideast 'peace talks' in Annapolis shun Hamas, do not raise Gaza

Unable to crush the Palestinian spirit with hunger, isolation and blockade, Washington is giving full support to political and diplomatic measures that would create an apartheid state.

The greatest attention has been paid to dividing the Palestinian movement with repression, mass imprisonment and torture of those who are determined to stand for their full rights. This is matched with empty promises to those willing to conciliate.

Hamas, the democratically elected Palestinian government, was not invited to an orchestrated photo-op in Annapolis, Md., in late

November 2007, held to supposedly discuss "peace and a Palestinian Homeland." Israel has refused any discussion or negotiation with Hamas forces.

U.S. Congress presses Egypt to seal Gaza tunnel lifeline

Before their winter holiday recess, both houses of the U.S. Congress agreed to withhold $100 million in financial assistance to Egypt, demanding that Egypt first take further steps to repress Palestinians who smuggle supplies and weapons into Gaza via a network of tunnels along the Egyptian border and clamp down on Gaza in other ways.

This heavy-handed pressure tactic is the first time that U.S. aid to Egypt—provided since the 1979 Egypt-Israel Camp David peace agreement—has been threatened and significantly reduced.

Now several thousand Palestinian pilgrims are stranded in Egypt. The Egyptian government has refused to let them return to the Hamas-controlled border city of Rafah in Gaza directly through Egypt.

The Gaza residents arrived in Egypt's Sinai Peninsula the last week in December after completing the Hajj in Mecca. They had left Gaza via Egypt on their way to the Hajj. However, Israel is demanding that the pilgrims pass through an Israeli-controlled crossing on their way back to Gaza so that Israeli forces can stop and interrogate suspected militants and their sympathizers.

It is important that the world movement stand with and give full attention to the Palestinian struggle. The onerous conditions of starvation and isolation of Gaza can only be broken by world solidarity.

Gazans stage 'biggest jailbreak ever'

Palestinians lift siege by blowing up 7-mile wall bordering Egypt;
700,000 Gazans walk into Egypt to buy supplies

By Joyce Chediac
Published Feb. 3, 2008
The following is based on a talk given at a New York City Workers
World Forum on Jan. 25, 2008.

The whole world watched in wonder when, on Jan. 23, 2008, the blockaded Palestinian people of Gaza blew up the walls imprisoning them and walked en masse into Egypt.

It was the biggest jailbreak ever.

In a bold challenge to Zionism, U.S. and European imperialism and neighboring reactionary Arab regimes, hundreds of thousands of men, women and children, many flashing victory signs, poured over, around and through the demolished wall into Egypt to get the food, medicine and other survival supplies they had been denied. There was no stopping them. [According to BBC, by Jan. 26, 700,000 Palestinians had crossed into Egypt, approximately half of Gaza's 1.5 million people, and they were still coming. —JC]

After getting what they needed to survive, the people turned around and went back to Gaza, to defend Palestinian land and continue the struggle.

Imperialism's weakness: It cannot defeat a people's movement

The people of Gaza have exposed the fundamental weakness of imperialism, Zionism and their local agents. The huge military colossus of the U.S. and Israel can hurt but cannot defeat a people's movement. The whip of repression—the daily Israeli bombardments and supply, food and medicine shortages—did not quell the people or consume their struggle.

On the contrary, the Palestinian population responded to the terrible six-month siege of Gaza with a new determination, raising the struggle to a higher level. This remarkable development is testimony to the strength of a mass movement and a bold leadership responsive to the people's needs.

Gaza's mass defiance gives heart to all under the iron heel of imperialism and capitalism.

Palestinians refuse to be starved into abandoning Hamas

U.S., Israel and the European Union hoped to pummel, starve, freeze and sicken the Gaza population into turning against Hamas, which it elected. This has backfired. Today, the prestige of Hamas is higher than ever. The Jan. 23, 2008, *New York Times* interviewed all classes of Palestinians breaching the wall, including Fatah supporters. All said, "This was the best thing that Hamas did."

Further isolated are the forces of Mahmoud Abbas, which are seen as aligned with the U.S. and Israel, and which attended Washington's so-called peace conference at Annapolis in January 2008, where the siege of Gaza was not even on the agenda. On Jan. 24, 2008, Hamas leaders called for unity and invited Abbas and the Ramallah government to run the Rafah border crossing into Egypt jointly with Hamas. So far, Abbas has refused this offer.

Israel turns Gaza into a new Warsaw ghetto

Israel's blockade and siege of the 1.5 million Palestinians in Gaza began in June 2007, when Hamas took over the government there. This punishment of the civilian population because Israel, the U.S. and the European Union did not like Gaza's government was a blatant violation of the Geneva Conventions governing the treatment of an occupied people, and a war crime.

Gaza became a new Warsaw ghetto. Unable to get supplies or export goods, the civilian economy collapsed, leaving the majority jobless and dependent on U.N. food handouts for survival. Gazans died because their medicines were no longer available. There was hunger, then starvation. And, all this time, the small strip of land was bombarded by Israel, using high-tech U.S. weapons.

Then, on Jan. 17, 2008, Israel shut off fuel shipments, plunging Gaza into darkness and rendering hospitals ineffective.

Hamas responded by organizing daily demonstrations at the closed Rafah crossing into Egypt, demanding that the border be opened. On Jan. 22, 2008, a demonstration of Palestinian women in traditional dress was beaten bloody by Egyptian security as they sought to cross the border and buy food and medicine for their families. (BBC, Jan. 22, 2008) The people had had all that they would take.

17 explosions rip through concrete and metal wall

In the wee dark hours of Jan. 23, 2008, 17 explosions ripped through the concrete and corrugated metal wall with Egypt. Most of the seven-mile wall blockading Gaza came tumbling down. While Hamas did not take credit, the Jan. 24, 2008, *London Times*, after interviewing Gaza residents, determined that this was not only a Hamas action, but the moment had long been planned. For months, the *Times* said, Hamas had been secretly slicing through the heavy metal portions of the wall with oxyacetylene torches.

Residents were told to stay away from the wall the night the explosions went off, the *Times* said.

The next day, a Hamas spokesperson would not take credit for exploding the wall. "We are creating facts," he said, adding, "We warned the Egyptians yesterday that people are hungry and dying." Hours later, the wall was demolished. (*New York Times*, Jan. 24, 2008)

Gaza's people and leadership united

Blowing up the wall was a bold move that spoke to the needs of the people. Gaza's residents did not have to be coaxed to cross. In fact, they couldn't be held back. Some 350,000 crossed the first day, with Hamas forces acting as guides.

They crossed over on foot, by donkey cart, in beat-up pickup trucks. While most went to purchase needed food and supplies, some went to see relatives, living in Egypt on the other side of Rafah, whom they hadn't seen in months. Some young people had never been out of Gaza, and they came just to breathe the air and feel free.

They returned carrying sacks of flour, with cans filled with olive oil and gasoline, with medicine, cigarettes and with carts filled with cement. They walked farm animals and camels into Gaza, giving the "V" for victory sign when news cameras were spotted. When Egypt used water cannons and riot police to close the two main border crossings on Jan. 27, 2008, Palestinians bulldozed another hole in the fence and used a crane to hoist needed goods over the barrier.

Egyptian security stood by, with many guards showing clear sympathy with the Palestinians and others overwhelmed by the sheer numbers crossing over.

Bush blocks U.N. condemnation of Israel for blockade

Just a few weeks ago, with much fanfare, the Bush administration held a conference at Annapolis and claimed it wanted a resolution to the Palestinian question. Washington's response to events in Gaza makes it clear that Washington is no friend of the Palestinians. On Jan. 23, 2008, the U.S. was the only U.N. Security Council member to oppose a statement condemning Israel for the blockade of Gaza.

Why? Turning events on their head, Washington insisted that the criminal and genocidal blockade of Gaza was an act of Israeli self-defense, because Palestinians in Gaza continue to fire homemade rockets into Israel. Surely, the rocket firers would gladly trade these homemade rockets for the laser-guided cruise missiles and "Apache" helicopters the Pentagon gives to Israel.

Hamas: 'We stopped the rockets, but the siege didn't end'

Speaking from Syria on Jan. 24, 2008, Khaled Mershaal, the head of Hamas's political bureau, explained: "The siege was before and after the firing of rockets. We stopped firing rockets many times, but the siege had not come to an end; we ceased the resistance tactically for several months, but the aggression and occupation continued." (Palestine Information Center, Jan. 24, 2008)

The breaking of the blockade of Gaza is a continuation of other mass actions in the Middle East.

For example, in 2000 Hezbollah and allied fighters liberated south-ern Lebanon from a decade of Israeli occupation. Their success was due to their deep roots in and support from the population.

In the summer of 2006, less than 3,000 Hezbollah people's fighters stopped the heavily armed Israeli army in its tracks, preventing it from invading Lebanon.

Today in Iraq and Afghanistan all the might of the Pentagon cannot stop the resistance, because these movements have the support of the people, and, in fact, are the people.

The Bush administration, aided by the establishment media, has tried to hide the mass character of these struggles. Nothing, however, could hide the fact that the breaching of the wall between Gaza and Egypt was done by the Palestinian people themselves.

IV

Israel Begins Air, Ground and Sea Assault on Trapped Gaza Population

On 27 December 2008, without warning, Israeli forces began a devastating bombing campaign on the Gaza Strip code-named 'Operation Cast Lead.' Its stated aim was to end rocket attacks into Israel by armed groups affiliated with Hamas and other Palestinian factions. By 18 January 2009, some 1,400 Palestinians had been killed and large areas of Gaza had been razed to the ground.

—Amnesty International report entitled "Israel/Gaza: Operation Cast Lead: 22 days of death and destruction."

The conventional rendition is that Israel invaded Gaza at the end of 2008 in order to stop a near-constant stream of rockets fired by Hamas. This history signals to readers that Israel was merely reacting to intolerable and persistent acts of violence. But that is wildly misleading. For much of the second half of that year, a truce between Hamas and Israel largely eliminated rocket fire from the Gaza Strip into Israel; the remaining handful of rockets were launched by rival Palestinian groups. That cease-fire was essentially shattered on November 4, when an Israeli incursion killed several Hamas members (Guardian, 11/5/08). Efforts to renew the cease-fire failed, and the ensuing violence culminated in the full-scale Israeli invasion.

—Fairness and Accuracy in Reporting, Jan. 6, 2009. FAIR is a media watch group.

U.S. paved way for Israel's attack

By Deirdre Griswold
Published Jan. 7, 2009

The response of the world's imperialist governments to Israel's ferocious assault on the 1.5 million Palestinians packed into Gaza shows once again who is really calling the shots in Tel Aviv. Israel has created a desperate humanitarian crisis in Gaza that will be felt for decades to come. Israel has violated many international laws regarding military violence against civilians. It has violated its own agreements with the Palestinians.

Yet nothing has been done by the "international community" to stop it. Significant opposition to this monumental crime comes from the streets, not the suites.

No other small country gets such kid-glove treatment. But Israel is not just a small country. It is a strategic partner of the world's lone superpower, the United States.

Israel keeps Mideast "safe" for U.S. oil company exploitation

The U.S. ruling class reaps hundreds of billions of dollars in profit from the exploitation of Middle East oil. If any government there tries to defend its sovereignty and gain greater control over its own resources, Israel is usually the first to threaten military action, as it has done with Iran. And it gets the favors that Washington bestows on its mercenaries: an average $15 million a day in military and economic aid (*Washington Report on Middle East Affairs*, September 2003) plus unlimited credit and access to priceless wheeling and dealing.

With Washington behind them, the Israeli rulers know there will be no U.N. Security Council resolutions to stop the carnage. No neighboring Arab countries will be able to come to the defense of their brothers and sisters without making themselves targets of the same U.S. planes, U.S. tanks and U.S. bombs now ripping apart the people of Gaza.

The Palestinians in Gaza had already been under a tight economic blockade for 18 months. Everything was in desperately short supply, including food, medicines, hospital equipment, fuel for heat, cooking, transportation and generators. Electric power was available only a few hours each day—the rest of the time there were no lights, no way to recharge cell phones or radio batteries, no working pumps for water. Sanitation barely functioned.

White phosphorus dropped on people with nowhere to hide

And then, on Dec. 27, 2008, Israel began its bombardment from the air. Using F-16s and "Apache" helicopters supplied by the U.S., it systematically targeted places where people might seek shelter.

One week later, on Jan. 3, 2009, its tanks and troops rolled across the border into Gaza's cities and towns, preceded by the raining down of white phosphorus from the air.

Phosphorus is so fearsome that it was banned as a weapon of war in civilian areas in the Geneva Treaty of 1980. It burns at high temperatures and adheres to flesh so tightly that, if even a small blob lands on a person's skin, it will burn right through to the bone. The U.S. used phosphorus and napalm against the Vietnamese people, prompting charges of war crimes. It is made in the USA.

Israel claims the phosphorus bombs were used only to create a "smokescreen" in advance of its ground troops. Its foreign minister, Tzipi Livni, said at a press conference in Paris on Jan. 3, 2009, the day the ground invasion started, that Israel had been careful to protect civilians and there was no need for a humanitarian truce, since there was no humanitarian crisis.

U.N. school bombed

In the first week and a half of their offensive, the Israelis killed an estimated 560 people and wounded thousands more. The U.N. relief agency says at least a quarter were civilians. But that number soared to more than 600 dead on Jan. 6, 2009, when Israeli mortars fell in a crowd of 350 people who had gathered for safety around the United Nations school in the Jabaliya refugee camp, killing at least 40, according to medical officials on the spot. (*Reuters,* Jan. 6, 2009)

The Israelis claimed the refugees had fired on them, but a U.N. official confirmed that no one in the crowd had weapons. The Israelis have bombed and/or shelled residential buildings, marketplaces, mosques, hospitals and other schools, including the prestigious American International School.

'The size of the operation and the size of the misery is overwhelming'

Israel has put a noose around Gaza and drawn it tight. It refuses to allow news media into the strip. However, the Arab news service *Al-Jazeera* was able to interview residents of Gaza after the ground assault began.

Iyad Nasr of the Red Cross in Gaza City told *Al-Jazeera*, "The size of the operations and the size of the misery we are seeing here on the ground is just overwhelming."

John Holmes, head of the U.N. Relief Agency, said in response to Israel's claims: "This is, in our view, a humanitarian crisis. It's very hard for me to see any other way you could describe it, given the conditions in which the population are living."

Holmes added that "cluster munitions are being used" and that many of the civilians killed were women and children. (*Al-Jazeera*, Jan. 6, 2009)

The *Sydney Morning Herald* on Jan. 5, 2009, published an eyewitness report from Shifa hospital in Gaza City—one of the few such first-hand accounts to appear in a major newspaper outside the Arab world.

Taghreed El-Khodary wrote: "The casualties at Shifa on Sunday [Jan. 4, 2009]—18 dead, hospital officials said, among a reported 30 around Gaza—were women, children and men who had been with children. One surgeon said he had performed five amputations."

Nurse at Shifa hospital: 'There is so much amputation'

"'I don't know what kind of weapons Israel is using,' said a nurse, Ziad Abd al Jawwad, 41, who had been working 24 hours without a break. 'There is so much amputation.' ...

"For 10 days doctors have been battling to keep Shifa running. Cleaners constantly mop up blood while Hamas security officers stand guard. ...

"Mads Gilbert, a Norwegian doctor who was allowed into Gaza last week to give emergency medical aid, and who has worked in many conflict zones, said the situation was the worst he had seen. The hospital lacked everything, he said—monitors, anesthesia, surgical equipment, heaters and spare parts. Windows had been blown out by a bombing nearby and like the rest of Gaza, limited fuel supplies were running low."

Israel uses 'bunker busters' made in USA

And now another fearsome weapon has been added to Israel's arsenal, thanks to Washington. The *Jerusalem Post* reported on Dec. 30, 2008, that Israeli pilots had dropped GBU-39 "bunker-buster" bombs on Gaza in the current offensive. In September 2008, the U.S. Congress approved the sale to Israel of 1,000 of these weapons, whose concentrated explosive power is eight times that of a conventional bomb.

Such transactions are called sales but in fact amount to grants, since Washington has allowed Israel to run up a huge external debt without calling in its chips. Today, Israel's foreign debt is equal to 99 percent of its gross domestic product. Half of this is owed to the U.S. (*CIA World Factbook*)

The Israelis say these bombs have been used to blow up tunnels in Gaza in the current offensive. They say their goal is to stop the smuggling of weapons. But the tunnels have been used to bring in needed supplies, so blowing them up has the effect of reinforcing the blockade of Gaza.

Myth of Gaza rocket 'threat' and Israeli 'defense' exposed

The Israeli propaganda machine, aided enormously by the supposedly "objective" U.S. media, tries to present this blitzkrieg as defensive—a needed action against rockets fired from Gaza into Israel by militants of Hamas. The figures, however, speak for themselves.

While in the first 10 days more than 500 Palestinians were killed and thousands more wounded, just four Israelis were killed by rockets. The number of dead Israelis doubled after the ground invasion started—but only because four of its soldiers were wasted by fire from their own tanks as they searched residential buildings in northern Gaza. (*New York Times*, Jan. 6, 2009)

Washington blocks U.N. call for ceasefire and carnage continues

The Bush administration is blatant in its support for this blitzkrieg. On Jan. 3, 2009, it prevented even the mildest call for a cease-fire from being voted on in the U.N. Security Council.

It is totally hostile to Hamas—the party leading the resistance, which was elected overwhelmingly by the Palestinian people in their last parliamentary vote. A recently revealed internal U.S. document shows that the U.S. secretly pledged $86 million to "strengthen and reform elements of the Palestinian security sector" in opposition to Hamas, thus trying to pit Palestinian forces against each other. (*Reuters*, Jan. 5, 2009)

Noting that this U.S. administration will be gone soon, some of his critics are calling Israel's assault "Bush's last war crime."

They are hoping for a less bellicose foreign policy under Barack Obama, who has so far refrained from commenting on Israel's air assault and invasion.

The position of both the Democratic and Republican parties, however, is all-out support for Israel as a racist settler state on Palestinian land. The rationale given is the assumption that Israel is the only place, since the Nazi Holocaust of World War II, where Jewish people can be safe.

Why Palestinians, a largely pastoral people who played no role in the crimes of German imperialism, should have to pay the price for them is never addressed.

Huge income disparity shows Israel no "homeland"

Also seldom mentioned is the dismal truth that many Jews in Israel, as well as the great majority of the Palestinians who live there, suffer deep poverty. In fact, of all the countries in the developed world, Israel comes in second-worst for income inequality. Which country is first? The United States. (*BBC News*, March 27, 2006)

Israel's National Insurance Institute found in 2007 that one in every four Israelis lives below the poverty line. For children, it is even worse. Some 35 percent of Israeli children are in poverty—ranking it among the Western countries with the greatest percentage of poor children. At the same time, the number of Israeli millionaires per capita is twice the world average, according to the 2005 World Wealth Report. (*The Jewish Journal*, March 8, 2007)

Senior Holocaust survivors, Arabs, suffer worst poverty

The situation in Jerusalem is even worse, with "62 percent of Arab families living below [the] poverty line compared to 23 percent of the city's Jewish families. Seventy-six percent of Arab children and 44 percent of Jewish children live in poverty in Jerusalem." (*Ha'aretz*, Jan. 24, 2008)

Among those Israelis suffering poverty at the hands of its billionaire-controlled government are seniors, including many of the Holocaust survivors still alive.

In recent years, as Israel's constant wars have gobbled up ever more state funds, its social services have been cut way back.

Israel is an artificial political creation, imposed on Palestine in 1948 by U.S. and British imperialism in a maneuver with the reactionary Zionist movement. For the good of all the peoples of the area, Washington must stop its financing and arming of this lawless and oppressive regime.

Hamas political leader:

'This brutality will never break our will'

Published Jan. 15, 2009

The following statement by **Khaled Mershaal**, *head of the Hamas political bureau, was published in* The Guardian *of Britain on Jan. 6, 2009.*

For 18 months my people in Gaza have been under siege, incarcerated inside the world's biggest prison, sealed off from land, air and sea, caged and starved, denied even medication for our sick. After the slow death policy came the bombardment. In this most densely populated of places, nothing has been spared by Israel's warplanes, from government buildings to homes, mosques, hospitals, schools and markets. More than 540 have been killed and thousands permanently maimed [as of Jan. 6—editor]. A third are women and children. Whole families have been massacred, some while they slept.

'Israel broke the ceasefire repeatedly from the start'

This river of blood is being shed under lies and false pretexts. For six months we in Hamas observed the ceasefire. Israel broke it repeatedly from the start. Israel was required to open crossings to Gaza and extend the truce to the West Bank. It proceeded to tighten its deadly siege of Gaza, repeatedly cutting electricity  and water supplies. The collective punishment did not halt, but accelerated—as did the assassinations and killings. Thirty Gazans were killed by Israeli fire and hundreds of patients died as a direct effect of the siege during the so-called ceasefire. Israel enjoyed a period of calm. Our people did not.

When this broken truce neared its end, we expressed our readiness for a new comprehensive truce in return for lifting the blockade and opening all Gaza border crossings, including Rafah. Our calls fell on deaf ears. Yet still we would be willing to begin a new truce on these terms following the complete withdrawal of the invading forces from Gaza.

No rockets have ever been fired from the West Bank. But 50 died and hundreds more were injured there last year at Israel's hands, while its expansionism proceeded relentlessly. We are meant to be content with shrinking scraps of territory, a handful of cantons at Israel's mercy, enclosed by it from all sides. The truth is Israel seeks a one-sided cease-fire, observed by my people alone, in return for siege, starvation, bombardment, assassinations, incursions and colonial settlement. What Israel wants is a gratuitous ceasefire.

'Our modest homemade rockets are our cry of protest to the world'

The logic of those who demand that we stop our resistance is absurd. They absolve the aggressor and occupier—armed with the deadliest weapons of death and destruction—of responsibility, while blaming the victim, prisoner and occupied. Our modest, home-made rockets are our cry of protest to the world. Israel and its American and European sponsors want us to be killed in silence. But die in silence we will not.

What is being visited on Gaza today was visited on Yasser Arafat before. When he refused to bow to Israel's dictates, he was imprisoned in his Ramallah headquarters, surrounded by tanks for two years. When this failed to break his resolve, he was murdered by poisoning.

Gaza enters 2009 just as it did 2008: under Israeli fire. Between January and February of last year 140 Gazans died in air strikes. And just before it embarked on its failed military assault on Lebanon in July 2006, Israel rained thousands of shells on Gaza, killing 240. From Deir Yassin in 1948 to Gaza today, the list of Israel's crimes is long. The justifications change, but the reality is the same: colonial occupation, oppression and never-ending injustice. If this is the "free world" whose "values" Israel is defending, as its foreign minister Tzipi Livni alleges, then we want nothing to do with it.

'Gaza's people are more united than ever'

Israel's leaders remain in the grip of confusion, unable to set clear goals for the attacks—from ousting the legitimately elected Hamas government and destroying its infrastructure, to stopping the rockets.

As they fail to break Gaza's resistance the benchmark has been lowered. Now they speak of weakening Hamas and limiting the resistance. But they will achieve neither. Gaza's people are more united than ever, determined not to be terrorized into submission. Our fighters, armed with the justice of their cause, have already caused many casualties among the occupation army and will fight on to defend their land and people. Nothing can defeat our will to be free.

Once again, Washington and Europe have opted to aid and abet the jailer, occupier and aggressor, and to condemn its victims. We hoped Barack Obama would break with George Bush's disastrous legacy, but his start is not encouraging. While he swiftly moved to denounce the Mumbai attacks, he remains tongue-tied after 10 days of slaughter in Gaza. But my people are not alone. Millions of freedom-loving men and women stand by its struggle for justice and liberation—witness daily protests against Israeli aggression, not only in the Arab and Islamic region, but worldwide.

Israel will no doubt wreak untold destruction, death and suffering in Gaza. But it will meet the same fate in Gaza as it did in Lebanon. We will not be broken by siege and bombardment, and will never surrender to occupation.

V

Israel Withdraws and Gaza Lives On, Bloodied but Unbowed

On Jan. 18, 2009, after three weeks of attack, Israel began a unilateral withdrawal from Gaza, unable to impose a formal cease-fire or conditions on Gaza. Instead, Tel Aviv unilaterally declared a cease-fire on Jan. 17, followed by a unilateral cease-fire declaration by Hamas 12 hours later, on Jan. 18. This was a humiliation for the Israeli government. Despite its vast firepower, its command of the air and the sea, despite the suffering inflicted by an 18-month blockade, Israel could not make Hamas or the people of Gaza admit defeat. Though it aimed its guns mostly on Gaza's civilians, Israel was unable to turn the people of Gaza against Hamas. Israel did not achieve its stated goal of ending Hamas's military capacity and stopping Gaza rockets, which continued to be fired into Israel up to the Hamas-declared cease-fire.

The people have won the most uneven of battles

By Deirdre Griswold
Published Jan. 21, 2009

The Palestinian people, bloodied but unbowed, have won the most uneven of battles.

The brutal scenario cooked up in the war rooms of the Israeli military and the Pentagon didn't work.

Palestinian Tahani Hijji, 26, carries her young child as she arrives to inspect her destroyed house in the southern part of Gaza City, Jan. 20, 2009.

The 22-day blitzkrieg against the people of Gaza and their democratically chosen leadership, Hamas, was supposed to break their spirit. Instead, it united the Palestinians more than ever against their oppressors and brought tears and roars of support from around the world.

The attackers seemed to have everything on their side:

• Highly trained troops bristling with the latest weapons.

• Total command of the air and sea around the tiny Gaza Strip, which is crowded with 1.5 million Palestinian refugees.

• An 18-month-long blockade that allowed the Israelis to turn off food, fuel, medicine and water like shutting a spigot.

• The complicity of all the imperialist powers, especially the U.S. Washington supplies Israel with weapons and money for its death machine, let it become a nuclear power, and has blocked any international action that even whispered criticism of the racist Israeli settler state.

• A Western-dominated world corporate media that, with few exceptions, sides with Israel.

Israel unable to impose ceasefire conditions on Gaza

Yet by Jan. 20, 2009, most of Israel's troops had withdrawn from Gaza without a formal cease-fire, meaning without Tel Aviv being able to impose conditions on the Palestinians. A coalition of resistance groups—including Hamas, Islamic Jihad, al-Nidal and al-Saeqa—had two days earlier announced a unilateral cease-fire on the condition that the Israelis withdraw within a week.

As the troops withdrew, aid workers were finally able to search the rubble for bodies. The destruction imposed by the invading troops and by air strikes had been horrendous.

Not a war but a massacre: Israel admits targeting ambulances

Preliminary figures reported by the Palestinian National Authority were that more than 1,400 Gazans were confirmed killed, more than 80 percent of them civilians, including over 300 children, and more than 5,000 wounded, according to Al-Haq, the Palestinian human rights group. Property damage in Gaza was estimated at $2 billion. By contrast, Israel lost 13 people, 10 of whom were soldiers. Yet the corporate media decry "violence on both sides."

Even with a cease-fire, the death toll of Palestinians continues to rise as decaying corpses are found in the shattered remains of buildings. They had lain there for days because the unadmitted policy of the Israeli military was to target rescue workers. It was reported that 13 medical workers were killed by the Israelis—most shot down while trying to recover civilian casualties.

Other atrocity stories are finally making it to the outside world.

Residents of the village of Khuza'a in southern Gaza told reporters for a London newspaper (*Observer*, Jan. 18, 2009) what had happened there during a sustained 12-hour assault by Israel.

"Israeli soldiers entering the village attempted to bulldoze houses with civilians inside; killed civilians trying to escape under the protection of white flags; opened fire on an ambulance attempting to reach the wounded; and used indiscriminate force in a civilian area and fired white phosphorus shells," survivors had reported.

Civilians mowed down in Khuza'a

In one incident, Israeli troops ordered 30 residents to leave their homes and walk to a school in the village center. After they had gone about 60 feet, troops fired on the group, killing three, the survivors said.

"If the allegations are upheld, all the incidents would constitute breaches of the Geneva conventions," continued the article. "The denunciations over what happened in Khuza'a follow repeated claims of possible human rights violations from the Red Cross, the U.N. and human rights organizations. ..."

"Pictures taken by photographer Bruno Stevens in the aftermath show heavy damage—and still-burning phosphorus. 'What I can tell you is that many, many houses were shelled and that they used white phosphorus,' said Stevens yesterday, one of the first Western journalists to get into Gaza. 'It appears to have been indiscriminate.' Stevens added that homes near the village that had not been hit by shell fire had been set on fire." (*Observer,* Jan. 18, 2009)

Amnesty International said on Jan. 19, 2009, that delegates it sent to Gaza had found "indisputable evidence of widespread use of white phosphorus in densely populated residential areas in Gaza City and in the north." The use of white phosphorus as a weapon in civilian areas is banned by international law.

DIME—another ghastly new U.S. weapon

Doctors in Gaza have also reported catastrophic injuries they believe were caused by another terrible new weapon: a Dense Inert Metal Explosive, or DIME device. The Pentagon began developing these weapons in 2006, but before Gaza their only suspected use had been by the Israelis during their attack on Lebanon that year.

Two European doctors working in the Gaza Strip—Jan Brommundt, a German with Medecins du Monde, working in the south Gazan city of Khan Younis, and Erik Fosse, a Norwegian surgeon at the Shifa hospital in northern Gaza—told *Al-Jazeera* that surgeons were encountering massive organ and tissue damage yet could find no evidence of shrapnel or other hard substances having entered the body. Both said they and their colleagues suspected a DIME explosive had been used.

A DIME device, explains the news service, "expels a blade of charged tungsten dust that burns and destroys everything within a four-meter radius.

"Brommundt also described widespread but previously unseen abdominal injuries that appear minor at first but degenerate within hours, causing multi-organ failure.

"'It seems to be some sort of explosive ... that disperses tiny particles ... that penetrate all organs,' the doctor said. 'Initially everything seems in order ... but they will present within one to five hours with an acute abdomen which looks like appendicitis but it turns out on operation that dozens of miniature particles can be found in all of their organs,' he said. The doctor added that these injuries can't be addressed surgically and that many patients succumbed to septicemia and died within 24 hours."

Dr. Fosse also told *Al-Jazeera* there had been a significant increase in double amputations. "We suspect they [Israel] used DIME weapons because we saw cases of huge amputations or flesh torn off the lower parts of the body," he said. "The pressure wave [from a DIME device] moves from the ground upwards and that's why the majority of patients have huge injuries to the lower part of the body and abdomen." Fosse said that most of the patients he saw with these injuries were children. (*Al-Jazeera*, Jan. 19, 2009)

War widened gap between the streets and the suites

Israel tried to make the best of its withdrawal, saying it had been timed for the inauguration of Barack Obama as the new U.S. president. Whether true or not—the Israeli military had originally said it would stay in Gaza as long as it took to destroy the Hamas leadership—this explanation reveals Israel's complete dependence on Washington.

While some critics of Israel claim it controls U.S. policy, the truth is that the ruling establishment in the U.S. has built Israel into a military bastion to counter the rising wave of national liberation struggles in the Middle East. Whether under secular or Islamic leadership, these mass struggles seek sovereignty and control over their national resources after more than a century of being plundered and demeaned by colonialism and imperialism.

If Washington thought that its support for this onslaught by Israel would advance its fortunes elsewhere—Iraq, Afghanistan, Pakistan—by spreading intimidation and fear, it now has to think again. The gap between the streets and the suites, especially in those Arab countries allied to the U.S., has never been greater.

Arab client regimes of U.S. feel people's anger

Anger and frustration have been rising, especially against the rulers of Egypt and Saudi Arabia, who are seen as traitors to the Arab cause. The Saudi monarch, King Abdullah, got much media attention when he tried to buy some credibility at a recent summit in Kuwait by pledging $1 billion to the reconstruction of Gaza.

At the same time, an international forum was being held in Beirut to build solidarity and practical support for the Palestinian cause among secular leftist and Islamic anti-imperialist forces. Forum participant Sara Flounders of the International Action Center told *Workers World*: "What was most significant about this major international gathering, taking place as Gaza was burning, was that it provided an international pole of resistance in sharp contrast to the U.S./Israeli pole of collaborators.

"Major countries opposing U.S. policy—including Lebanon, Venezuela, Iran and Syria—sent top delegations that gathered with leaders of the most active anti-war and Palestine solidarity groupings whose mobilizations had brought millions into the street.

"It was clear to all that at a great cost of blood and sacrifice, Palestinians in Gaza had prevailed. Israel had not succeeded in disarming or gaining the surrender of Hamas.

"The struggle continues into a new period more confident and more connected."

Hamas calls war:

'Decisive loss for Israel'

Published Jan. 28, 2009

The following essay by Mousa Abu Marzook, deputy chief of the Hamas political bureau, was published in the Guardian *on Jan. 22, 2009.*

Israel's objectives from the war on Gaza were set long before its launch: to remove the Hamas movement and government, achieve the reinstallation of the Fatah leader, Mahmoud Abbas, in Gaza, and end the armed resistance. Two other objectives were not announced. First, restore the Israeli public's wavering confidence in its armed forces after its defeat by Hezbollah [in Lebanon] in 2006. Second, boost the coalition government in the coming elections.

Accordingly, we declare that Israel lost, and lost decisively. What did it achieve? The killing of large numbers of civilians, children and women, and the destruction of homes, ministry buildings and other infrastructure with the most advanced United States weapons and other internationally banned chemical and phosphorous elements. ... Many international organizations called these attacks war crimes, yet barely a word of denunciation was uttered by any Western leader. What message does the European Union mean to send Palestinians by its shameful silence on these crimes, when it speaks incessantly on human rights?

European leaders should recognize election they called for

If anything, the last three weeks, and previous 18 months, have proved that the Palestinians can never be broken by either starvation, economic strangulation or brutal attack. European leaders have only one option: to recognize the outcome of a democratic process they had called for and supported.

The aggression failed to undermine or weaken the Hamas-led government, or turn Palestinians against Hamas. If anything, public support is stronger than ever in Palestine and worldwide. Hamas's military capabilities have not been hurt, either. This explains Israel scurrying to sign such a strange agreement with the U.S. to stop arms reaching Hamas. It is doomed to fail. As the former Israeli chief of staff Moshe Yaalon and [right-wing Likud party leader] Benjamin Netanyahu agreed, Israeli forces failed to achieve their objectives.

Why is Israel allowed a continuous flow of the most lethal arms, including banned weapons, while national resistance movements are denied the means of defense? International laws permit occupied nations to resist their occupiers, and that is a right we aim to utilize to the full.

Israel must accept the reality that it is incapable of breaking the Palestinian resistance. Similarly, Europe must accept that bringing back Abbas on an Israeli tank is not an option. Nor are attempts to win by "diplomacy" what the might of the Israeli military failed to secure by force. To state that all aid for Gaza reconstruction must go through the illegal government of appointed Palestinian Authority Prime Minister Salam Fayyad suggests there is no end to some parties' exploitation of Palestinians. We will never cease to pursue national unity, but we will never allow it to be attained by compromising Palestinian rights.

Sderot built on ransacked Palestinian village

And to President Obama we say: The wave of hope that met your election was heavily dampened by your silence on the Gaza massacre. This was compounded by your pre-election statement siding with the Israeli settlers of Sderot. You would do well to know the history of the places of which you speak. Sderot, which may be known to some as an Israeli town, lies on the ruins of Najd, a Palestinian village ransacked in May 1948 by Zionist terrorist gangs. Villagers were forced from their beds and homes with nothing but the clothes they were wearing, rendering them refugees for the next 61 years. That is the story of Sderot. It is never a good start to get your tyrant and victims mixed up, but there is still room for a revival of passionate optimism. Only if you decide to fairly address the issue of the 6 million Palestinian refugees and the ending of occupation of Palestinian lands, including Jerusalem, will you be able to start a new relationship with the Muslim world.

Life-sustaining corridor:

Tunnels of Gaza are a symbol of resistance

By Sara Flounders
Published Feb. 8, 2009

Resistance takes as many forms as life itself dictates.

Life in Gaza could not be more impossible. Its tunnels are a symbol of resistance.

Eighteen months ago, outraged when the Palestinians voted for the militant leadership of Hamas in democratic elections, Israel imposed a total lockdown on the entire population of Gaza.

But the entire people were determined to continue to resist. They found a way to circumvent total starvation.

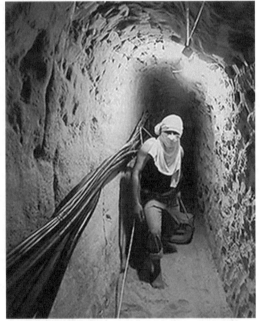

1,000 tunnels dug under sealed border

The Israeli blockade led to a new economic structure, an underground economy. The besieged Palestinians have dug more than 1,000 tunnels under the totally sealed border.

Many thousands of Palestinians are now employed in digging, smuggling or transporting, and reselling essential goods. Smuggling constitutes approximately 90 percent of economic activity in Gaza, according to Gazan economist Omar Shaban. (*Guardian*, Oct. 22, 2008)

The tunnels demonstrate the great ingenuity and enormous determination of the entire population and its leadership.

Because millions of Palestinians have been forced into refugee status outside of historic Palestine, large extended families on both sides of the border help arrange the buying and shipping of goods or send funds so family members locked in Gaza can buy essential supplies.

Life-sustaining corridor

The tunnels connect the Egyptian town of Rafah with the Palestinian refugee camp of the same name inside Gaza. They have become a fantastic, life-sustaining network of corridors dug through sandy soil. Tunnels are typically three-tenths of a mile long, approximately 45 to 50 feet deep. They cost from $50,000 to $90,000 and require several months of intense labor to dig.

They pass under the Philadelphi buffer zone—a border strip of land put under Israeli military control by the 1993 Oslo accords.

The Israeli siege of Gaza, followed by 22 days of systematic bombing and invasion, has created massive destruction and scarcity. Food-processing plants, chicken farms, grain warehouses, U.N. food stocks, almost all the remaining infrastructure and 230 small factories were destroyed. Now hundreds of trucks packed with essential supplies from international and humanitarian agencies sit outside the strip, refused entry to Gaza by Israeli guards. As soon as the Israeli bombing ended, work on the tunnels resumed.

Banks of red earth crisscross no-man's land

Lara Marlowe reported from Rafah: "From a distance, you'd think it was a horticultural project. Banks of red earth crisscross the Palestinian side of the no-man's land between Gaza and Egypt. Every 20 or 30 meters, young Palestinian men work under what appear to be greenhouse canopies.

"The tunnels of Rafah—more than one thousand of them—are a major stake in the war between Hamas and Israel. Israel wants the tunnels shut; the Palestinians say they would starve without them, because of Israel's 19-month siege of the Gaza Strip. Despite three weeks of heavy bombing, the majority of the tunnels are open.

"The area has as many holes as a Swiss cheese. 'Sometimes the tunnels intersect,' says a worker. 'We try to avoid it. We go under or over other tunnels. It's like directing train traffic.'

"The smugglers work in jeans, T-shirts and bare feet. 'We shore up the collapsed parts with wood,' Hamdan [a tunnel worker] explains. 'If the Israelis bomb again, we'll use metal next time, and concrete the time

after that. As long as there's a siege, the tunnels will keep working.'"
(*Irish Times,* Jan. 26, 2009)

On Egyptian side, sympathetic guards look the other way

Food is towed through on plastic sleighs. Livestock are herded through larger tunnels. Flour, milk, cheese, cigarettes, cooking oil, toothpaste, small generators, computers and kerosene heaters come through the tunnels. Every day, about 300 to 400 gas canisters for cooking come through the lines. On the Egyptian side the trade sustains the ruptured economy while corrupt or sympathetic guards and officers look the other way.

Electricity and fans provide ventilation. Essential supplies of diesel fuel are pumped through the tunnels in hoses and pipes.

Rami Almeghari, editor-in-chief of the Gaza-based *Palestinian Information Service* and contributor to *The Electronic Intifada*, has described the organization that goes into digging and maintaining the tunnels. The Hamas-led government in Gaza imposed regulations and restrictions on the tunnel trade to avoid accidents and prevent smuggling of drugs and prohibited substances. "However, the besieged Hamas government cannot guarantee an end to the tunnel trade, unless the Israeli blockade comes to a halt."

Almeghari interviewed one tunnel worker as he loaded cooking oil canisters: "Let Israel besiege us the way it wants, and we bring in what we want. At the end of the day, we will not let anyone repress us."

Xinhua News headlined a Jan. 22, 2009, article: "In spite of Israeli offensive, Gaza tunnels are back to work."

'We have no other alternative'

"We dug tunnels because we have no other alternative. Israel was imposing a very tough blockade on Gaza Strip and the tunnels were the smartest way to defeat this blockade," Hashem Abu Jazzar, a 23-year-old worker, told *Xinhua News.*

"As long as Israel is still imposing the siege on Gaza Strip, I don't think that we will stop working in the tunnels, but if all crossings are fully and permanently opened, I believe that working in tunnels will automatically stop," said Abu Jabal, a 45-year-old owner of a tunnel.

Commercial tunnels are used only for food, fuel, medicines and basic necessities. Other totally separate tunnels are operated by resistance groups to bring in small weapons and munitions.

Israel claims it drops 100-ton bombs on the tunnels from F-16 jets to stop Palestinian rockets. But closing off supplies to an entire population or bombing life-sustaining tunnels will not prevent the firing of small rockets.

A population with skills, education, massive unemployment, lots of time and no future will be able to build rockets, mortars, pipe bombs and mines out of the tons of scrap metal and twisted ruins that Israel left behind.

The continued blockade is strictly punitive.

Massive bombardment couldn't close lifeline

The Israeli military and their Pentagon backers are deeply frustrated. The bombing failed to demoralize the Palestinian people or break their will. It is also clear that the massive bombardment of the Rafah border and the targeting of hundreds of tunnels have failed to close these lifelines of basic supplies.

On Feb. 1, 2009, Israel again bombed the border, targeting the tunnels.

What is needed is a broad international campaign to demand an end to U.S.-supported Israeli collective punishment and an end to the intended starvation of an entire population.

The only possibility for peace in the region is through the recognition of the full rights of the Palestinian people to return to all their land. Their sovereignty and economic development must be guaranteed.

VI

A Movement Grows
in Solidarity with Gaza

*Even while Israeli bombs rained down on Gaza civilians, the world's
powerful governments sided with Israel, contributed to the economic
strangulation of Gaza, and ignored the suffering there. But the people in
these countries heard Gaza's cry for help. The horror of the Israeli
onslaught, the bravery of the Palestinians in Gaza, and the continued
inaction of the big powers sparked first outrage, then action in solidarity with
Gaza across the globe.*

Seoul, South Korea

People worldwide protest
U.S.-Israeli massacre

Vienna, Austria

By John Catalinotto
Published Dec. 31, 2008

The U.S.-backed Israeli bombardment of the Palestinian people in the Gaza Strip has had at least one unintended consequence. It has mobilized the anti-imperialist movement and other anti-war forces around the world.

The Washington-Tel-Aviv axis might not yet see this as an obstacle. But it is a work in progress, coming as the workers' movements are beginning to get in motion to fight the repercussions of the capitalist economic collapse. Now they are fighting to stop the Israeli massacre in Gaza.

Tel Aviv   Photo: Jessie Boylan

Even in parts of the world where winter holidays often drain the strength of a social movement, people reacted quickly, angrily and in some places massively to oppose the new Israeli assault.

Groups all over the world made strikingly similar calls for action. There was complete solidarity with the Palestinians of Gaza, a besieged and occupied population that has every right to resist. Most saw the Israeli state as the direct criminal, the local gendarme acting as an appendage of world imperialism—particularly U.S. imperialism but also that of the European Union.

The immediate demands were to stop the Israeli attacks; lift the blockade of Gaza; and for the government involved to break relations with or stop aiding the Zionist state. Protests in some mostly Arab countries—Egypt, for example—also targeted the country's regime for collaborating with the U.S. and Israel. Disrupting the stability of the collaborating Arab regimes could be another unwanted consequence of the U.S.-Israeli assault.

People began to hit the streets and squares in protest the day of the first Israeli bombing, Dec. 27, 2008. Demonstrations spread through Asia, Africa, Latin America, Europe, Canada and the U.S. in the next few days.

In addition to these popular actions, statements from the governments of Cuba, Venezuela and Bolivia condemned the Israeli killing of Palestinians.

Outraged demonstrations
in every major U.S. city

Buffalo, New York   WW Photo: Leslie Feinberg

By Cheryl LaBash
Published Jan. 5, 2009

Outraged demonstrations to stop what is seen by many here as a "U.S./Israeli bombing of Gaza" flared in every major U.S. metropolitan area more than once, and in some cases, daily.

At Israeli consulates, offices of U.S. senators and representatives, and at busy street corners, Palestinian and Arab organizations are being joined and supported by anti-Zionist Jewish, anti-war, African-American, Latina and Latino, Asian and labor organizations. Below are some highlights.

Filled with anguish and anger, 25,000 to 30,000 people rallied in New York City's Times Square on Jan. 3 in one of the largest U.S. protests. This demonstration was called right after U.S.-made Israeli tanks rolled into Gaza in a full ground invasion.

However, scores of demonstrations were called around the country as soon as the bombs began falling on Gaza on Dec. 27, 2008, including a protest of 1,500 in Anaheim, Calif., on Dec. 29.

In Washington, D.C., on Jan. 2, several thousand people rallied at the Israeli Consulate and marched to the Egyptian Consulate to charge complicity in the Gaza blockade. That same day in Chicago 5,000 protesters packed into Pioneer Plaza. It was the fifth pro-Gaza Chicago action in a week.

On Jan. 2 nearly a thousand people of diverse ethnic and religious backgrounds gathered at the Dearborn, Mich., City Hall in frigid temperatures to hold a solidarity candlelight vigil. The next day a thousand chanting pro-Palestinian demonstrators lined a busy intersection in suburban Detroit.

A thousand people gathered in Dallas on Jan. 2, and a thousand more in Houston. Hundreds took to the streets every day for a week in Austin, Texas.

On Jan. 3, about 1,000 people stretched across the steps in front of Philadelphia's City hall with a banner "War is Terrorism with a Bigger Budget—Stop the U.S.-Israeli War on Palestinians."

That same day in Boston, about 1,500 chanting, "From the river to the sea, Palestine will be free!" and "We support the resistance!" marched through that city's main shopping area, stopping at the U.S. military recruiters' office and the Israeli Consulate.

San Diego, California

WW photo:
Bob McCubbin

Ramsey Clark petition against bombing and siege draws strong response

A petition posted online right after the bombing began offered an early opportunity to oppose Israel's attack on Gaza. This "Urgent Appeal for Israel to Immediately Cease Its Murderous Bombing, Siege and Invasion of Palestinian Gaza" was initiated and written by Ramsey Clark, a former U.S. Attorney General and U.N. Human Rights Prize recipient who has represented the Palestine Liberation Organization in U.S. courts.

The petition was circulated by the International Action Center (www.IACenter.org) nationally and internationally in several languages, including Spanish and Arabic

The many thousands of people who signed this petition generated approximately 500,000 protest e-mails. Each signer directed their protest to President Barack Obama, Secretary of State Designate Hillary Clinton, Vice President Joe Biden, Congressional leaders, U.N. General Assembly President d'Escoto-Brockmann, U.N. Secretary General Ban Ki-moon, members of the U.N. Security Council, U.N. member states, the President, Prime Minister, Cabinet and Opposition leader of Israel, and major media representatives:

"Through most of the recent years Israel has attacked Fatah," the petition stated. "Now it is Hamas that Israel attacks. ... Israel's policy has always been to destroy the possibility of a Palestinian State. Its criminal assault on Hamas is in truth Israel's continuing assault on the possibility of a Palestinian State [through] divide and conquer."

The petition called upon:
The U.N. and world governments "to demand an immediate ceasefire throughout Israel and Palestine and the assurance of peace. All borders to Gaza – with Israel, Egypt and the Mediterranean Sea – must be opened for humanitarian relief and a complete arms and trade embargo imposed on Israel until it fully complies with all the requirements of permanent peace....

"All the people, the ultimate power in every nation when organized and energized, to take to the streets where they live and demand that their governments do all in their power to cause Israel to stop its war of aggression against Palestine and for all parties to pursue peace and for Israel, the U.S. and other nations who have provided material support for Israel's aggression to be held accountable for the deaths, injuries and damage Israel has inflicted....

"Governments and humanitarian agencies to provide all needed emergency relief to Palestine – medical care, food, humanitarian supplies, shelter; and on all the media that truly seeks peace, justice and respect for the equal dignity of every child, woman and man on earth to headline the demand that Israel stop its aggression immediately. All parties must engage in continuous negotiation with all Palestinians until a one-state solution is agreed or the state of Palestine as mandated not later than October 1948 in U.N. General Assembly Resolution 181 (1947) is created, fully implemented, and Palestine thrives."

Support for Gaza is not charity

The U.S. government gives Israel $3 billion in military aid each year. This same money, if used to meet human needs at home, could provide 24 million uninsured people with primary health care services, or give 364,000 low-income households affordable housing vouchers, or retrain 498,000 workers for green jobs, or create early reading programs to 887,000 at-risk students.
    —U.S. Campaign to End the Israeli Occupation

Excerpted from a Workers World Party statement published Jan. 5, 2009
    The workers' movement of the entire world should leave no doubt that it stands on the side of the Palestinian resistance, and will give unconditional support to whatever the Palestinians need to do to defend the people of Gaza and their organizations, which includes Hamas.

World outcry against onslaught
    How then to best take the side of the people of Gaza and their elected government? The world's people are showing how. Within hours of the initial U.S.-Israeli bombing attack on Dec. 27, 2008—that's U.S. planes, helicopters, bombs and rockets and Israeli pilots—people all over the world, including in the United States, began demonstrating in solidarity with the Palestinians. After the land invasion, hundreds of thousands came out again in hundreds of world capitals and smaller cities and towns.
    Many of the initial protesters were Palestinian or other Arab and Muslim people who are now living in exile all over the globe. But where the workers' and anti-war movements were strong, these forces also joined the Palestinians. This has begun to happen also in the United States, and everything must be done to increase this solidarity with Palestine.
    This is not charity. It is not only out of sympathy with Gaza's suffering people. It is mutual solidarity with the heroic Palestinian struggle against the common enemy. For the working class, too—not only in the "global South" but also in Europe, Japan and the United States—has been under attack. Its jobs have disappeared, its wages diminished, and its social services cut. The workers have begun fighting defensive battles and can identify with the defensive struggle of the Palestinians.

A political activist in Texas, recently thanked for her assistance at a series of protests by the Palestinian community, put it this way: "Yes, I'm in solidarity with Palestine, but I also don't want my tax money used for bombs and war planes instead of education for my grandchildren. We have the same enemies."

New York City, Dec. 28.

She got an answer: "You have a point. I'm Palestinian, but I'm also a Houstonian. My services, my children's services are cut. I need to fight those local battles, too."

A Hamas leader recently called for a "Third Intifada," referring to the two heroic and determined mass uprisings of the entire Palestinian population, the first beginning in 1987 and the second in 2000, both of which lasted for years and which left as their legacy the pictures of Palestinian children throwing stones against the Israeli armored vehicles.

Bring spirit of Palestinian people's struggle to movements here

What then is the strongest way to express international solidarity? By joining the workers' struggle right here in the defense of Palestine and bringing the spirit of the Palestinian struggle for national liberation—the Intifada—into the workers' and anti-racist movement. This would be the best way to turn the taste for conquest into bitter ashes in the mouths of Bush, Cheney, Olmert, Barak and Livni.

Jews in solidarity with Palestine

By Shelley Ettinger
Published Jan. 21, 2009

As the world watched the continuing Israeli bombing and invasion of Gaza in horror, as angry protests continued around the globe, a group of Jewish people inside the U.S. took a public stand in support of the Palestinian people and against the Zionist settler state.

A Jan. 14, 2009, statement issued by the International Action Center on behalf of Jews in Solidarity with Palestine said: "No to Israel! Yes to self-determination, democracy and freedom!

Jewish group shuts Israeli Consulate in Los Angeles to stop slaughter in Gaza.

Photo: Robert Lowden

Stop the U.S.-backed genocidal Israeli war on Gaza! Stop U.S. funding of the war on Palestine!"

The statement says Israel's war on Gaza "reflects the program of the Israeli settler state—which is based on the theft of Palestine, the ouster and suppression of the Palestinian people, and the racist ideology of Zionism." It continues: "It's not enough to oppose the bombing. It's not enough to demand an end to the 41-year occupation of Gaza and the West Bank.

"We stand in complete and unconditional support for the self-determination of the Palestinian people. This includes the right to return to Palestine, from the river to the sea, and the right to democratically determine the form and future of the Palestinian state."

The JSP statement calls the creation of Israel "a crime [that] betrayed the whole history of the Jewish people," noting that "from helping topple the czar in Russia and build the unions in New York, to resisting pogroms and fighting to the last breath in the Warsaw Ghetto, opposition to persecution, oppression and racism was central to the Jewish heritage."

It calls on "Jewish people around the world, including those inside Israel, to join us in reclaiming that heritage. Reject racism and genocide. Reject the Zionist state, the very concept of which is racist to the core. Take the hand of our Palestinian sisters and brothers. Defend their righteous struggle to restore their stolen land and build a democratic Palestine."

The appeal struck an immediate chord. Hundreds of people responded within hours of the statement going public. In three days, over 1,100 people had added their names as signers or endorsed the JSP statement. The names are still pouring in.

The signers include a survivor of the Nazi holocaust, a child of Holocaust survivors, a 1933 refugee from Hitler Germany, and even a resident of an Israeli kibbutz. Messages of support and thanks from non-Jews also arrived.

Jewish actions vs. Israel

The JSP statement and the strong response to it are one indication that the Zionist state's longtime lock on Jewish loyalty is no longer absolute. Anguished and shamed by the horrors of U.S.-backed Israeli crimes against the Palestinian people, more Jewish people are rethinking their support for Israel.

In Los Angeles on Jan. 13, 2009. a group of Jewish activists blockaded the Israeli Consulate to protest the Gaza atrocities. They chained themselves together and blocked access to the building.

An open letter from Jewish people to Israeli soldiers is circulating worldwide. It characterizes Israel's operation in Gaza as a war crime and calls on the soldiers to refuse orders to take part.

Another letter, signed by 78 Jewish people, primarily academics, in England, says, "The time for appeasing Israel is long past," and demands, "Britain must withdraw the British ambassador to Israel and, as with apartheid South Africa, embark on a program of boycott, divestment and sanctions."

Inside Israel, another protest against the Gaza war was set for Jan. 17, 2009, in Tel Aviv, and some Israeli troops and officers, known as "refuseniks," have resisted duty in Gaza.

Martin Luther King Day
turns toward Palestine

Martin Luther King Day, Los Angeles

January 15, 2009, marked the 80th birthday of civil rights leader Martin Luther King Jr. The King commemoration fell during the bombing of Gaza. Across the country, many African-American communities opened up their King Day events, and their hearts, to the Palestinian community and to the people of Gaza.

By Betsey Piette
Published Jan. 21, 2009

The largest and loudest contingent in Atlanta's annual Martin Luther King Day march was that of Palestinians and other opponents of the U.S.-backed Israeli massacre in Gaza. The lead banner quoted King, "Injustice Anywhere is a Threat to Justice Everywhere," followed by "Let Palestine Live!" A hundred supporters of Gaza braved the freezing cold to march in the annual King Parade in uptown Charlotte, N.C. They received overwhelming support from the mainly African-American spectators along the route.

Detroit's King Day stressed solidarity with the Palestinian people of Gaza and invited speakers from the Arab-American community. A delegation from Cleveland's Palestinian community joined the King Day march there to the police department, courts and Cuyahoga County jail to protest racial disparities in sentencing, police brutality and mistreatment in the jail. Inmates banged on their windows, held up lettered signs and waved clothing in solidarity. In New York City, a Palestinian-initiated demonstration of 3,000 protesting the punishment of Gaza also commemorated Dr. King, chanting "No justice! No peace!"

Some 10,000 people marched in the annual King event in Seattle. Three big banners demanded freedom for Palestine. Hundreds in San Diego expressed outrage against the U.S.-funded Israeli attacks. In Los Angeles, King Day protesters joined Black community leaders at a news conference condemning the U.S.-Israeli massacre in Gaza. Speakers included Hank Jones of the San Francisco 8 and representatives from the Black UCLA student organization ASAP, Global Women's Strike, All African People's Revolutionary Party, KPFK radio and the International Action Center. They demanded that Barack Obama and Black elected officials in Congress meet their historical obligations to fight injustice by ending their silent complicity and work towards ending all aid to Israel.

'If they come for Gaza in the morning they will come for Harlem at night'

By Abayomi Azikiwe
Editor, Pan-African News Wire
Published Jan. 21, 2009

Although many people within the United States, from various nationalities and cultures, have expressed solidarity with the Palestinian people since the Israeli aerial bombardment of Gaza started on Dec. 27, the bourgeoisie stills refuses to allow an open debate around the question of an independent state for this oppressed people. At the same time the ruling elites have set out to shape political opinion in favor of imperialist aims in the Middle East.

One key tactic in the ruling-class effort to build support for imperialist aims in the Middle East is to openly solicit collaboration between African-American political and religious leaders and the state of Israel. During the early phase of the bombing of Gaza by the Israeli Air Force, the Detroit City Council president, Monica Conyers, traveled to Israel to supposedly study the conflict in occupied Palestine.

In 2008, a well-known African-American minister, Kenneth Flowers, pastor of the Greater New Mount Moriah Baptist Church in Detroit, was invited to Israel in order to receive a "Martin Luther King" award. Flowers took a delegation of several African Americans with him on the trip to Israel, which included the president of the Detroit-Metro AFL-CIO, Saundra Williams.

Bishop Keith Butler of the World of Faith Ministries has hosted public meetings in support of Israel. Glenn Plummer, head of the Christian Television Network (CTN), openly speaks in favor of the Zionist regime and U.S. foreign policy in the Middle East.

In two Congressional votes on a nonbinding resolution endorsing the Israeli genocidal onslaught against the Palestinian people on Jan. 8 and 9, 2009, the U.S. Senate voted unanimous support of the Zionist military program against the Palestinians. In the House of Representatives, only five members voted against a similar resolution.

Among the approximately 40 members of the Congressional Black Caucus, only two voted against the resolution supporting Israel. Yet, despite these efforts to influence the elected political leadership and selected African-American religious figures, most working-class and poor Black people in the U.S. oppose the government's hostility toward the Palestinian people.

Civil rights, Black liberation movements identified with Palestinians

This defiance can be traced back to the period of the rising civil rights and Black liberation movements of the 1960s and 1970s. The most advanced political elements within these movements saw a direct relationship between the national oppression suffered by people in the U.S. and the struggles of the Palestinians and other colonized people in other parts of the Middle East and the world.

One of the major conflicts that would shape and define the post-World War II period was the establishment of the state of Israel in 1948 and the resulting displacement and occupation of the Palestinian people. Interestingly enough, one African American, Ralph Bunche, a Harvard-educated political scientist, was intimately involved in the imperialist machinations that led to the creation of the Israeli regime, despite his own misgivings about the creation of the state of Israel and how harmful he knew it would be for Palestinians.

Malcolm X on Palestine

By the 1960s, revolutionary African-American leaders such as Malcolm X, through his involvement in the Nation of Islam and the later Organization of Afro-American Unity (OAAU), openly criticized Zionism as a political philosophy and expressed solidarity with the struggle of the Palestinians and the Arab national liberation movements throughout the region.

In an article by Malcolm X published on Sept. 17, 1964, in the *Egyptian Gazette*, he pointed out that the Zionist regime in Palestine served U.S. imperialist aims in the Middle East and Africa.

After the assassination of Malcolm X in February 1965, the youth elements within the civil rights movement became more radicalized. The Student Nonviolent Coordinating Committee (SNCC) issued a statement in opposition to the U.S. war against Vietnam in January

1966, becoming the first major civil rights organization to openly call for the end of the war and the elimination of the draft.

SNCC supports Arabs in 1967 war

In 1967, during the Arab-Israeli so-called "Six Day War" in June, SNCC took a position in support of Egypt and the other Arab states, as well as the Palestinians. The organization came under fire once again for opposing U.S. foreign policy.

James Forman, who in 1967 served as the international affairs director for SNCC, wrote in his political autobiography, "We were too radical then, for not supporting domestic policies of the administration, and we were too radical now—for opposing American foreign policy, for seeing Israel as an imperialist power in the service of, and serving, that policy." (*The Making of Black Revolutionaries,* Forman, p. 496)

Another SNCC leader, Stokely Carmichael (later known as Kwame Ture), delivered a major address at the Organization of Arab Students conference held at the University of Michigan in August 1968. In this speech, Carmichael reiterated the organization's position in support of the Palestinian struggle and also discussed the role of Zionist ideology inside the U.S.

Carmichael said: "What makes the forces of Zionism so effecttive in their propaganda is that the Zionists have something else: not only do they assert theirs as a fact, and anyone who questions it they put on the defensive by calling him anti-Semitic, but the Zionists hook up the killing of six million Jews as a justification for the so-called state of Israel.

"They say, 'Six million Jews were murdered by Hitler; we have a right to Israel.' And that is a very dangerous thing. It is a fact that six million Jews were slaughtered by Hitler, but that six million Jews were murdered by Hitler does not give the Zionists the right to take Arab land." (*Stokely Speaks,* 1971, 2007, p. 137)

This position in support of the Palestinian struggle was also adopted by other revolutionary organizations such as the Black Panther Party and the League of Revolutionary Black Workers. By the late 1970s, even more centrist African-American leaders sought to intervene in resolving the Palestinian question.

Andrew Young ousted for speaking to
Palestine Liberation Organization

Even the United Nations ambassador for the U.S. under the Carter administration, Andrew Young, who was a former civil rights leader who worked alongside Martin Luther King Jr. in the Southern Christian

Leadership Conference (SCLC), was removed from his position in the Carter administration in large part because of his efforts to open up dialogue with representatives of the Palestine Liberation Organization (PLO) at the U.N.

In the aftermath of the removal of Andrew Young in 1979, another civil rights leader who had also worked with Dr. King, Rev. Jesse Jackson, took a trip to the region and developed a position calling for dialogue with the Palestinians.

With the advent of Barack Obama's candidacy for president in 2008, the senator from Illinois went to great lengths not only to express his support for the pro-Israel position, as reflected in his major address at the American-Israeli Political Action Committee conference in early 2008, but also to stay clear of any substantive discussion involving the Palestinian struggle for self-determination and statehood. Obama has surrounded himself with pro-Israel aides, including his secretary of state, former Sen. Hillary Clinton, and his chief of staff, Rahm Emanuel, who, according to news reports, served in the Israeli military.

Cynthia McKinney aboard humanitarian aid ship rammed by Israel

In contrast, former U.S. Rep. Cynthia McKinney, who ran for president on the Green Party ticket in 2008, supported the Palestinian people as part of a solidarity delegation which sought to deliver aid to the people of Gaza, who had been under a blockade for months.

McKinney was a passenger on the *Dignity* vessel, which was denied entry into Gaza in December 2008 by the Israeli Navy. The *Dignity* was hit and damaged by the Israeli military forces. McKinney, in subsequent interviews, stated that she felt her life was in danger during

Cynthia McKinney

the ordeal with the Israeli Navy. Undeterred, she maintains her support for the right of self-determination for the people of Palestine.

'Liberation struggles of the oppressed must not be divided'

During the latest assault on Gaza, there has been a groundswell of support and sympathy in the U.S. for the Palestinian people, especially among African Americans and other oppressed national groups.

The Blacks Against Genocide Coalition issued a statement that read in part: "We, Black people in the United States, condemn the criminal Israeli attacks on the people of Gaza. These war crimes are being conducted with the overt material and unapologetic political backing of the U.S. government."

This statement continues by pointing out that "Most importantly, we have learned the lessons of four centuries of racist oppression in the Western hemisphere: that the liberation struggles of the oppressed must not be divided by language, geography, gender, religion or race; that if they come for Gaza in the morning, they will most certainly come for Harlem at night."

African Americans and other oppressed sectors of the working class in the U.S. recognize that the deepening economic crisis is, at least in large part, a direct result of the militarism of U.S. imperialism. The ongoing wars of occupation in Iraq, Afghanistan, Somalia and Haiti have strengthened the repressive apparatus of the U.S.

Consequently, the liberation of African Americans and other oppressed peoples can only be won when imperialism is challenged and defeated in other parts of the world. Therefore, the defeat of imperialism in the so-called developing or Third World countries will inevitably advance the struggle for the total liberation of the oppressed and working people inside the imperialist states.

Anti-imperialists unite at Beirut Forum:

Secular and Muslim groups stand together for Palestine

By Bill Doares, Beirut, Lebanon
Published Jan. 21, 2009

As the people of Gaza staved off yet another attempt by the U.S.-armed and -funded Israeli military to eradicate the cause of Palestine by murdering its people, delegates from around the world gathered in Beirut to build solidarity and practical support for their cause among secular leftist and Islamic anti-imperialist forces.

Dr. Ali Fayyad, the director of the Consultative Center for Studies and Documentation in Beirut, who hosted the Beirut Forum, laid out its goals: "In this part of the world the resistance is Islamic. The resistance movement here must introduce themselves to other forces of resistance to imperialism around the world. The ideological differences must be postponed. The resistance must prevail. ... An important goal of the forum is to find how, despite the ideological contradictions, to work together hand in hand to achieve unity against imperialism."

The Beirut International Forum for Resistance, Anti-Imperialism, Solidarity Between Peoples and Alternatives, held from Jan. 16 to 18, 2009, assembled 450 international and Arab bodies, in addition to social movements and figures from 66 countries, on the soil of Lebanon, where the U.S.-created Israeli war machine suffered its first strategic defeat at the hands of the Lebanese Resistance in 2006.

Besides the host group, also participating was the National Gathering to Support the Choice of Resistance (Lebanon), in collaboration with the International Campaign against American and Zionist Occupation (the Cairo Conference), the International Anti-Imperialist and Peoples' Solidarity Forum (the Calcutta-India Conference) and the Stop War Campaign (London). Many hundreds of resistance organizations and prominent individuals endorsed the call for the Beirut Forum.

Manik Mukherjee, secretary general of the International Anti-Imperialist and Peoples' Solidarity Forum, who traveled for and worked on the Beirut Forum for the past year, headed an important delegation from India. The International League of People's Struggle also participated.

The largest number of delegates came from the Muslim and Arab world, including Iran and the Communist and Ba'ath parties of Syria, but there were also many from Latin America, including 30 from the Bolivarian Republic of Venezuela. Guests from Venezuela comprised members of parliament, unionists and youth from both the United Socialist Party (PSUV) and the Communist Party of Venezuela (PCV).

From Europe, besides the collaborating groups, members of the Party Red of Norway, Odiario.info of Portugal, the Anti-Imperialist Camp, workers' parties in Greece and Cyprus and many other anti-imperialists from around Europe attended.

Anti-war forces there from the U.S. included former congressional representative and presidential candidate Cynthia McKinney, former U.S. Attorney General Ramsey Clark and delegations from the International Action Center and the Freedom Road Socialist Organization. McKinney was recently on the ship *Dignity*, which was rammed by the Israeli Navy while trying to bring medical aid to Gaza. Sara Flounders, IAC co-director, addressed the Palestine Plenary Session.

'Unite leftist, secularist, committed Muslims and nationalists'

"There are two camps in the world, that of imperialism, led by the United States, and that of resistance," declared the Hezbollah deputy general secretary, Sheikh Naim Kassem, at the conference's opening session. "And I think the resistance camp will overcome." He called on fighters for freedom and justice around the world to follow the example of the Lebanese resistance: "We have united the leftists with the secularist, the committed Muslim and the nationalist. ... We should join hands to form a pressing and effective force, regardless of color, ethnicity, language, religion or creed."

Sheikh Kassem denounced Washington's attempts to impose "a market economy" on other countries. "People around the world find that their problems are caused by U.S. intervention, and we should unite. But there is no solidarity without support of resistance. ... Gaza today is the symbol of resistance and human dignity. We call upon you to stand with Gaza to scatter the darkness of imperialism and Zionism."

Speakers from Hamas, Gaza's democratically elected governing party, Islamic Jihad and the Popular Front for the Liberation of Palestine drew rousing applause from all assembled as they described the horrific suffering and heroic resistance of Gaza's people and called for political solidarity so that the people of Palestine would not lose diplomatically what they defended on the battlefield.

Panels and workshops combined political talks and action proposals with powerful personal testimony. Egyptian journalist Dalia Saladin described her visit to Gaza last January when freedom fighters forced open the Rafah crossing with Egypt. "Every household has at least one martyr and another disabled by the war. But when you walk among the people, you feel you have entered a new culture and a new social perspective, a culture of giving and sacrifice for others, where the poorest of the poor, especially mothers, set the example."

A Lebanese man, Hussein Shokr, brought delegates to tears when he told how an Israeli missile had killed his wife and four children during the 2006 war while he was away working in Canada.

Activists from Greece and Cyprus told of their efforts to break the blockade of Gaza physically and of how Greek dockworkers had refused to load U.S. arms bound for Israel.

In the conference closing session, Palestinian Resistance hero Leila Khaled of the Popular Front for the Liberation of Palestine spoke of the "unilateral ceasefire" just announced by Israeli forces. "We salute all those who fight to break the siege of Gaza. We affirm that this victory was won by our freedom fighters on the ground. The unilateral ceasefire proves that, with all its destructive capacity, Israel could not achieve its goals on the battlefield. They are now seeking the help of the United States to achieve those goals politically. But we consider occupation to be an act of war. When injustice is law, resistance is duty. And the only answer to occupation is resistance and liberation."

A prime organizer of the conference was Mohamed Kassem, a leader of the Lebanese teachers' union. "For the first time, in Lebanon," he said, "we have created a platform for struggling people all over the world, secular, nationalist, leftist and Islamic, to speak their views and work together, against the wars in Palestine, Iraq and Afghanistan, against the threats to Iran and the sanctions on Sudan, against the blockade of Cuba and the attempts to block the revolutionary direction in Venezuela, Bolivia and across Latin America. ... We are building mechanisms of international cooperation and South-South solidarity, and we plan to intensify those efforts in the future."

Palestine stands for global resistance

Published Jan. 21, 2009

The following is from a talk by Sara Flounders, co-director of the International Action Center, to the Palestine Plenary Session of the Jan. 16-18 Beirut International Forum for Resistance, Anti-Imperialism, Peoples' Solidarity and Alternatives.

The United Nations just stands by, the European Union is in full support of the Zionist state. From Saudi Arabia to Egypt to India, nations who were once considered friends of Palestine stand by and watch Gaza burn—day after day after day!

While the world's regimes watch Gaza burn

Why, why is this? The global inaction is because the rich and powerful are terrified of, and desperately want to destroy, resistance in their own countries. They want to destroy the glorious example of resistance—which Palestine represents to the whole world.

Every one of the great powers and their collaborators hope that by attacking Heroic Gaza they can push back and demoralize the struggle in the whole region.

Gaza is a harbinger of wider war against oppressed people of the world. We are on the eve of a global capitalist crisis. This means massive insecurity, cutbacks in all social programs, unemployment for millions.

Millions of working people will seek to fight back against a system of endless war and greater and greater dividends of enormous wealth for a handful and poverty for the overwhelming majority. Increasingly they will identify with and take heart from the many forms of resistance they see around them.

Gaza inspires struggles worldwide

For decades the Palestinian struggle has been the shining example to all the world of a people who refuse to submit to colonial domination, apartheid conditions, the most brutal forms of segregation and subjugation.

We need to make it clear that we support the right to resist, the right to fire rockets, the right to dig tunnels, the right to organize the people against sure starvation and the blockade that Israel has criminally imposed.

We need to militantly support Hamas, the democratically elected choice of the people, which is being demonized, hunted and assassinated by the Zionists, as is every heroic fighter.

At this forum we salute the powerful resistance of Iraq and the struggle waged by all of the different forces opposing U.S. occupation.

We salute the resistance in Afghanistan—a resistance that the U.S. never expected.

We salute the heroic forces in Lebanon, led by Hezbollah, which organized such a devastating setback to Israel in 2006.

We stand with the people of Syria and with Iran, who, in the face of U.S./Israeli threats, have been steadfast.

We applaud the people of Venezuela and Bolivia, who have shown such great solidarity with the struggle in Gaza as they organize to build a more just society.

Oppose NATO in Palestine, Egypt

Now we need to connect the criminal role of NATO in Afghanistan, NATO in the Balkans, in Georgia—to the phony Israeli cease-fire in Gaza. Washington now wants NATO military forces in Palestine and Egypt! NATO is the U.S. shield to do what Israel alone can no longer do. It is an effort to impose greater U.S. control in the region. But there is greater and greater resistance everywhere to these plans.

Organizers represented at this forum are involved in the most practical work of mobilizing opposition at the grassroots. Collectively we have brought millions into the streets in public demonstrations of solidarity. This is true in the Arab and Muslim world, through the entire South, and also in the imperialist countries. In some places we have blocked and even occupied the embassies of Israel and targeted countries that have collaborated with Israel's war crimes. Activists here today have taken boats to Gaza and taken up collections for people-to-people humanitarian aid.

From the U.S.—we are proud to have helped to organize many thousands of people in the streets, emergency demonstrations day after day for three weeks in New York, Los Angeles, Chicago and many other cities.

We must sustain an ongoing movement to boycott, divest and to impose sanctions (BDS) on the Israeli state and war crimes charges on its leaders. We must demand an accounting from our own governments.

Sisters and brothers—Gaza stands for global resistance. Palestine is fighting for all of us! We must fight for Palestine.

Caracas, Venezuela

VII

U.N. and Human Rights Reports and Israeli Soldiers' Testimony Expose War Crimes

"The death toll of Operation Cast Lead exceeded 1,400 Palestinians, 83 percent of whom were civilians, including 355 children; over 5,000 more were wounded."
> —Al-Haq, the Palestinian affiliate of the International Commission of Jurists

Thirteen Israelis lost their lives during Operation Cast Lead. Three civilians and one soldier were killed by rockets fired from Gaza. Nine Israeli soldiers were killed, four of them by friendly fire.
> —Figures provided by the Israeli government

The great disparity between the Palestinian and Israeli deaths resulting from Operation Cast Lead speaks volumes. However, even after the smoke cleared and the devastating damage to Gaza was documented, the Israeli regime continued to claim that it, and not Gaza, was the victim of aggression, that it acted in self-defense, and its targets in Gaza were military. This pretext was accepted and repeated by the U.S. and European powers and given validity in the media.

Two months after the 22-day war, however, Israeli Defense Forces soldiers who had participated in Operation Cast Lead began to come forward and give testimony confirming their government's policy of deliberately targeting the civilian population in Gaza, destroying the civilian infrastructure and killing non-combatants. Two articles here detail their testimony.

A month later, the Palestinian human rights organization Al-Haq explained exactly how Israel's claims of "self defense" distorted international law in an attempt to cover its naked aggression against Gaza. This report is excerpted here.

Six months after the war, a 574-page U.N. probe of the Gaza war and siege, known widely as the Goldstone Report, was released by the United Nations. It is a scathing indictment of Israeli policy and war crimes in Gaza. The executive summary of this report is excerpted here.

Israeli soldiers:

'Military command set tone for atrocities'

By Michael Kramer
Published March 29, 2009

The testimony was reminiscent of the Winter Soldier hearings that featured U.S. Iraq War veterans. In February 2009, Israeli Defense Forces (IDF) soldiers who took part in Operation Cast Lead, the military's name for its invasion of Gaza, described their experiences and observations. They had come together at the Oranim Academic College in Kiryat Tivon, where they had all attended a pre-military preparatory program as teenagers. The transcripts of their testimonies were released in mid-March.

On Dec. 27, 2008, the IDF launched a devastating U.S.-funded air, ground and naval attack against the Palestinian population of Gaza. Six months of detailed planning preceded the attack. In 22 days, more than 1,400 Palestinians—mostly civilians, including hundreds of children—were killed, thousands more were wounded and tens of thousands were left homeless.

Elders executed

At the hearings, "Zvi" described the execution of a Palestinian elder: "You see a person on a road, walking along a path. He doesn't have to be with a weapon, you don't have to identify him with anything and you can just shoot him. With us it was an old woman, on whom I didn't see any weapon." (*Ha'aretz*, March 19, 2009)

"Ram" recounted how a Palestinian mother and her two children were forced out of their home and told to go to the right. When they got confused and went to the left, they were all shot dead.

Intentional destruction of homes

Other Israeli soldiers described the intentional destruction of homes, furniture and personal property and how these crimes resulted from the tone set by their military command structure.

The testimonies are further evidence that the atrocities committed against the Palestinian people in Gaza during Operation Cast Lead must be labeled war crimes and that the criminals who planned and commanded this operation must be prosecuted as war criminals.

These war criminals include Prime Minister Ehud Olmert, Defense Minister Ehud Barak, Foreign Minister Tzipi Livni and military command personnel like Gabi Ashkenazi, Yoav Galant, Amos Yadlin, Hartzi Halevi, Yoav Mordechai and Yigal Slovik.

Middle-grade and high-ranking IDF officers are regularly rewarded with all-expenses-paid scholarships to U.S. universities for graduate study. Students and faculty should be on the lookout for the above-mentioned and other IDF war criminals. If identified, the school administration should be challenged about their presence on campus.

Zionist movement fractured

The steadfast and heroic Palestinian resistance to Zionist occupation now spans six decades. The resistance has resulted in one crisis after another in a Zionist movement that always had numerous contending and contentious factions (social democratic, fascist and religious, to name a few). Today the Zionist movement is more fractured than ever before. Weeks after a national election it still cannot form a coalition government to administer the so-called state of Israel.

Its armed wing, the IDF, is also feeling the stress and strain from a resistance to occupation it cannot defeat. This is resulting in growing numbers of youth refusing conscription and reservists refusing call-ups and deployments. In addition, there is a growing divide in the IDF between super-racist religious fundamentalists and more secular soldiers.

Troops call war crimes against Gaza Israeli 'policy,' demand accountability

By Dee Knight
Published July 23, 2009

A new publication by the group Breaking the Silence was announced on July 15, 2009. The group is composed of veteran Israeli soldiers who "demand accountability regarding Israel's military actions in the Occupied Territories perpetrated by us and in our name."

Interviews and testimony by 30 Israeli soldiers regarding their experiences in Operation Cast Lead confirm that war crimes were specific policy in last winter's Gaza massacre. The testimony, gathered in soldier-to-soldier interviews, began to surface in Israel shortly after the end of the December-January war.

Israel's leading newspaper, Ha'aretz, reported on March 20, 2009: "The soldiers describe the killing of innocent civilians, pointless destruction, expulsions of families from homes seized as temporary outposts, disregard for human life and a tendency toward brutalization."

Chain of command ordered 'widespread abuse'

London's Guardian reported March 22, 2009, that the testimony "suggests widespread abuses stemming from orders originating with the Israeli military chain of command." It adds that soldiers said they were "specifically warned by officers not to discuss what they had seen and done in Gaza."

The following are excerpts from that testimony:

"What shocked me was a talk we had with ... a colonel. Usually in such talks the commanders mention the lives of civilians and showing consideration to civilians. He didn't even mention this. Just 'go in there brutally.' He said, 'In case of any doubt, take down houses. You don't need confirmation for anything.'

"The instruction was explicit—if you're not sure, kill. The minute we got to our starting line, we simply began to fire at suspect places. ... You see a house, a window, shoot at the window. You don't see a terrorist there? Fire at the window. It was real urban warfare. ... In urban warfare, anyone is your enemy. No innocents.

"From the onset, the brigade commander and other officers made it very clear to us that ... if you see any signs of movement at all, you shoot. No consideration of civilians was to be taken."

Battle commander: 'Don't let morality become an issue'

"The battalion commander said, 'Don't let morality become an issue. That will come up later. ... It's not that you're out to carry out a massacre, but – .' This was the restraint to everything he had said before, and in between his own jokes. Like, 'We have an Arabic-speaking grenade launcher and a heavy machine-gun that speaks Arabic.'

"Our objective was to demolish houses. ... Houses were demolished everywhere. You see clearly that these houses had been fired at with tremendous power. We didn't see a single house that remained intact. ... The entire infrastructure, tracks, fields, roads, was in total ruin. ... Nothing much was left in our designated area. ... A totally destroyed city.

"This was fire-power such as I had never known. There were blasts all the time. The earth was constantly shaking. Explosions were heard all day long, the night was filled with flashes, an intensity we had never experienced before. ... The air force bombed all the time. ..."

White phosphorus 'fun'?

"Most of the mosques were demolished. That brigade commander I mentioned explicitly told us we should not hesitate to target mosques. Nothing is immune, nothing and no area. He explicitly mentioned mosques.

"Our battalion mortars were also using phosphorus. I know of an officer's tank that fired phosphorus, too. The company commander gives the mortar platoon commander a target and orders him to fire. ... They define targets. ... Sometimes you'd hear on radio, 'Permitted, phosphorus in the air.' That's it."

An interviewer asked the soldier: "Why fire phosphorus?"

"Because it's fun. Cool. ... I don't know what it's used for. I was just talking about this yesterday. I don't understand what it's even doing in our supplies if we're not supposed to use such ammo. It's ridiculous. In training you learn that white phosphorus is not used, and you're taught that it's not humane. You watch films and see what it does to people who are hit, and you say, 'There, we're doing it too.' That's not what I expected to see."

The full testimony is available at BreakingtheSilence.org.il.

Operation Cast Lead and the distortion of international law

"The thesis that the danger of genocide was hanging over us in June 1967 and that Israel was fighting for its physical existence is only bluff, which was born and developed after the war."
— Israeli Gen. Matityahu Peled, *Ha'aretz*, March 19, 1972

Israel, which has the fourth most powerful military in the world, still tries to justify its aggressions against the Palestinian and other Arab peoples as "self-defense." The following legal analysis of Israel's claim to self-defense under Article 51 of the U.N. Charter, excerpted from an April 2009 report by Al-Haq, shows how Israel has twisted international law to make this claim for Operation Cast Lead. Al-Haq is an independent Palestinian non-governmental human rights organization based in Ramallah, Occupied West Bank, and the West Bank affiliate of the International Commission of Jurists–Geneva.

In the morning hours preceding the initiation of ["Operation Cast Lead"], Israeli Ambassador to the U.N. Gabriela Shalev dispatched a brief to the U.N. Secretary-General announcing that "after a long period of utmost restraint, the government of Israel has decided to exercise, as of this morning, its right to self-defense ... as enshrined in Article 51 of the Charter of the United Nations."

The Israeli claim to 'self-defense' as the legal pretext for "Operation Cast Lead" received wide and generally unconditional support from the international diplomatic community as justification for the military assault against the Gaza Strip.

Israel's invocation of Article 51 of the U.N. Charter as the pretext for "Operation Cast Lead" is, however, based on two legally untenable assumptions. First, Israel maintains that the Gaza Strip is no longer occupied and therefore Israel bears no responsibility for the territory. Second, Israel's claim of self-defense fails to take into account the broader international armed conflict in which "Operation Cast Lead" was launched. Cumulatively, such assumptions distort the applicable framework of international law to the Occupied Palestinian Territory

(OPT), including the Gaza Strip, in an attempt to create a façade of legitimacy for the claim of 'self-defense' as the justification for "Operation Cast Lead."

Legal status of the Gaza Strip

Together with the West Bank, including East Jerusalem, the Gaza Strip is an integral and inseparable part of the Palestinian territory occupied by Israel since 1967. The OPT is recognized as a single territorial unit over which the Palestinian people's right to self-determination is enshrined in international law.

Israel, however, maintains that its unilateral disengagement from the Gaza Strip in 2005 relinquished its effective control over that part of the OPT, and in consequence the Gaza Strip is no longer occupied, effectively relieving Israel of its obligations under international humanitarian law as the Occupying Power. However ... the Gaza Strip remains under Israeli occupation.

Article 42 of the Hague Regulations of 1907 provides that, "territory is considered occupied when it is actually placed under the authority of the hostile army."

By declaring that "Israel will guard and monitor the external land perimeter of the Gaza Strip, will continue to maintain exclusive authority in Gaza air space, and will continue to exercise security activity in the sea off the coast of the Gaza Strip," the text of the "Disengagement Plan" itself reveals Israel's intention to maintain effective control over the Gaza Strip. Furthermore, despite the unilateral withdrawal of stationed troops and settlers, Israel continues to exert its military control over the Gaza Strip through a continuous flow of military operations in and against the Gaza Strip. (In addition to "Operation Cast Lead," "Operation Summer Rains" and "Operation Autumn Clouds" in 2006 and "Operation Hot Winter" in 2008 are among numerous large-scale Israeli military operations directed against the Gaza Strip since Israel's unilateral "disengagement.") ...

Israel also maintains administrative control over the population of the Gaza Strip through the exclusive control over the movement of goods and people, the civil population registry, and the tax and revenue system. Thus, the Gaza Strip and its inhabitants remain under Israeli effective control and, therefore, occupied. ...

Article 51 [of the U.N. Charter] ... provides that all States have the "inherent right of individual or collective self-defense if an armed attack occurs against a Member of the United Nations." Any use of force outside of these contexts is strictly prohibited. ...

'Operation Cast Lead' and international humanitarian law

"Operation Cast Lead," however, was launched within the context of a prolonged occupation [and therefore] the legal framework applicable to "Operation Cast Lead" is international humanitarian law, which regulates the conduct of hostilities during armed conflict and occupation. ... The ability for Israel to invoke Article 51 of the U.N. Charter as the legal pretext for "Operation Cast Lead" was excluded on 7 June 1967, the day the Palestinian territory came under the effective control and therefore occupation of the Israeli armed forces, rendering Israel the Occupying Power and bound by the provisions of the Fourth Geneva Convention.

As the Occupying Power, Israel bears specific legal obligations ... including the legal obligation to "ensure" adequate food and medical supplies and the functioning of medical, public health and hygiene services ... [and] to treat the occupied population, at all times and in all circumstances, humanely. ...

Military action must be intended towards the military defeat of the opposing forces and [is] restricted by the principles of distinction and proportionality. ... During military operations, Israel is obliged to ... direct its operations exclusively against military targets.

Furthermore, the principle of proportionality dictates that launching an attack, which may be expected to cause incidental loss of civilian life, injury to civilians or damage to civilian objects, which would be excessive in relation to the concrete and direct military advantage anticipated, is prohibited. ...

[Israel is expected to] take precautions in the choice of means and methods of attack with a view of avoiding and minimizing civilian casualties. ...

Contrary to such obligations, a prominent feature of "Operation Cast Lead" was disproportionate and often indiscriminate military attacks against densely populated civilian centers throughout the Gaza Strip. Al-Haq fieldworkers extensively documented the systematic failure of Israel to effectively distinguish between civilian and military objectives during attacks and a clearly identifiable lack of proportionality between the death and injury of civilians, destruction of civilian property and the concrete military advantage offered from such attacks. Indiscriminate and disproportionate attacks constitute war crimes;

where they result in willful killing and extensive unlawful destruction of property, such attacks may amount to grave breaches of the Fourth Geneva Convention, entailing individual criminal liability for those who planned, ordered or executed such operations.

Conclusion

Israel's reliance on self-defense misconstrues international law in an attempt to evade international legal obligations by failing to take account of the legal context in which "Operation Cast Lead" was launched: 42 years of occupation of the Palestinian territory equating to an international armed conflict. Despite the widespread acceptance of Israel's pretext, the legal status of the OPT excludes the application of Article 51 of the U.N. Charter as a result of the prolonged occupation. "Operation Cast Lead" cannot be isolated from the broader international armed conflict from which it was launched, a legal context where Israel's claim to self-defense holds no validity under international law.

The Goldstone Report:

U.N. probe is scathing indictment of Israeli policy

On Sept. 15, 2009, the United Nations Human Rights Council released the results of its "United Nations Fact-Finding Mission on the Gaza Conflict." This 574-page document became known as the Goldstone Report, after the man who headed the investigation, Justice Richard Goldstone, former judge of the Constitutional Court of South Africa, who is Jewish.

Based on 188 individual interviews, 10,000 pages of documentation, 1,200 photographs, including satellite imagery, and 30 videos and public hearings where 38 people testified, the report presents a strong case against Israel for committing war crimes during the invasion of Gaza and is a scathing indictment of Israeli policy.

The report also condemns the Palestinian armed groups, including Hamas, whose low-tech missiles, which could not be aimed, hit civilian areas in Israel. (It should be noted that during Operation Cast Lead, four people were killed in Israel by Palestinian missiles, three of them civilians, while more than 1,400 Gazans were killed by the IDF, 83 percent of them civilians.)

Hamas cooperated with the U.N. report, gave its investigators access to Gaza, answered all questions asked, and was ready to state its case and answer the charges against it. The Palestinian authority in the West Bank also cooperated with the Mission.

In marked contrast, the Israeli government refused to cooperate, denied U.N. investigators access to the areas it controlled, and ignored a list of questions posed to it by an investigator.

The U.N. report recommends that its findings be referred to the U.N. Security Council for further investigation, and if no action is taken, then be referred to the prosecutor of the International Criminal Court.

A struggle is being waged over this report. Virtually every Palestinian organization is fighting to bring the report to the International Court of

Justice, with the goal of trying Israel for war crimes, getting some justice for the people of Gaza, and imposing sanctions on Israel. Washington and Tel Aviv are fighting to bury this report so that it never reaches the court or any significant U.N. body.

Below are excerpts from the Executive Summary of the Goldstone Report.

The Gaza authorities report 1,444 fatalities. ... According to the Government of Israel, during the military operations there were four Israeli fatalities in southern Israel, of whom three were civilians and one a soldier. They were killed by rocket and mortar attacks by Palestinian armed groups. In addition, nine Israeli soldiers were killed during the fighting inside the Gaza strip, four of whom as a result of friendly fire. ...

Israel 'deliberately targeted civilians'

On 15 January 2009, the field office compound of the United Nations Relief and Works Agency for Palestine Refugees in the Near East (UNRWA) in Gaza City came under shelling with high explosive and white phosphorus munitions. ... The compound offered shelter to between 600 and 700 civilians and contained a huge fuel depot. The Israeli armed forces continued their attack over several hours despite having been fully alerted to the risks they created. ...

On the same day, the Israeli armed forces directly and intentionally attacked al-Quds hospital in Gaza City and the adjacent ambulance depot with white phosphorus shells. [Israeli armed forces staged] intense artillery attacks, again including white phosphorus munitions, on al-Wafa hospital in eastern Gaza City ... a violation of the prohibition of attacks on civilian hospitals.

[Israeli armed forces conducted] mortar shelling of al-Fakhura junction in Jabaliya next to a UNRWA school, which, at the time, was sheltering more than 1,300 people. ...

[Investigated were] 11 incidents in which the Israeli armed forces launched direct attacks against civilians with lethal outcome. ... The first two are attacks on houses in the al-Samouni neighborhood south of Gaza City, including the shelling of a house in which Palestinian civilians had been forced to assemble by the Israeli armed forces.

[Israeli armed forces were responsible for] the shooting of civilians while they were trying to leave their homes to walk to a safer place, waving white flags and, in some of the cases, following an injunction from the Israeli forces to do so. ... The consequences of the Israeli attacks against civilians were aggravated by their subsequent refusal to allow the evacuation of the wounded or to permit access to ambulances. ...

'Willful killing' of civilians violates Fourth Geneva Convention

These incidents indicate that the instructions given to the Israeli armed forces moving into Gaza provided for a low threshold for the use of lethal fire against the civilian population. ... From the facts ascertained in all the above cases, the Mission finds that the conduct of the Israeli armed forces constitutes grave breaches of the Fourth Geneva Convention in respect of willful killings and willfully causing great suffering to protected persons and, as such, give rise to individual criminal responsibility. It also finds that the direct targeting and arbitrary killing of Palestinian civilians is a violation of the right to life. ...

Phosphorus weapons used in high-density civilian areas

Based on its investigation of incidents involving the use of certain weapons such as white phosphorus and flechette missiles [an anti-personnel weapon whose shell explodes in the air and releases thousands of metal darts 37.5 mm in length] ... the Israeli armed forces were systematically reckless in determining its use in built-up areas. Moreover, doctors who treated patients with white phosphorus wounds spoke about the severity and sometimes untreatable nature of the burns caused by the substance. The Mission believes that serious consideration should be given to banning the use of white phosphorus in built-up areas. ... Flechettes [are] an area weapon incapable of discriminating between objectives after detonation ... [and] are ... particularly unsuitable for use in urban settings. ...

Attacks on the foundations of civilian life in Gaza

El-Bader flour mill was the only flour mill in the Gaza Strip still operating [after the siege. It] was hit by a series of air strikes on 9 January 2009. ... The precise targeting of crucial machinery suggests that the intention was to disable the factory's productive capacity. [This is] a violation of the grave breaches provisions of the Fourth Geneva Convention ... [as] the destruction of the mill was carried out to deny sustenance to the civilian population. ...

The chicken farms of Mr. Sameh Sawafeary in the Zeytoun neighborhood south of Gaza City reportedly supplied over 10 percent of the Gaza egg market. Armored bulldozers of the Israeli armed forces systematically flattened the chicken coops, killing all 31,000 chickens inside, and destroyed the plant and material necessary for the business. ...

Sewage processing plant bombing 'premeditated'

[The Israeli armed forces bombed] a wall of one of the raw sewage lagoons of the Gaza wastewater treatment plant, which caused the outflow of more than 200,000 cubic meters of raw sewage onto neighboring farmland. The circumstances of the strike suggest that it was deliberate and premeditated. The Namar wells complex in Jabaliya consisted of two water wells, pumping machines, a generator, fuel storage, a reservoir chlorination unit, buildings and related equipment. All were destroyed by multiple air strikes on the first day of the Israeli aerial attack. ...

[There was] destruction of residential housing caused by air strikes, mortar and artillery shelling, missile strikes, the operation of bulldozers and demolition charges. ... The Israeli armed forces engaged in another wave of systematic destruction of civilian buildings during the last three days of their presence in Gaza, aware of their imminent withdrawal. [This constitutes] destruction ... of property, not justified by military necessity and carried out unlawfully and wantonly. ...

There was a deliberate and systematic policy on the part of the Israeli armed forces to target industrial sites and water installations. ...

Gazans detained, degraded, exposed to elements

[The Israeli armed forces] rounded up large numbers of civilians and detained them in houses and open spaces in Gaza and, in the case of many Palestinian men, also took them to detention facilities in Israel. ... [N]one of the civilians was armed or posed any apparent threat to the Israeli soldiers. ...

Civilians, including women and children, were detained in degrading conditions, deprived of food, water and access to sanitary facilities, and exposed to the elements in January without any shelter. The men were handcuffed, blindfolded and repeatedly made to strip, sometimes naked, at different stages of their detention. ...

'Dahiya doctrine' of Lebanon war applied to Gaza

The incidents and patterns of events considered in the report are the result of deliberate planning and policy decisions. ...

The tactics used by the Israeli armed forces in the Gaza offensive are consistent with previous practices, most recently during the Lebanon war in 2006. A concept known as the Dahiya doctrine emerged then, involving the application of disproportionate force and the causing of great damage and destruction to civilian property and infrastructure, and suffering to civilian populations. [This is] precisely what was put into practice. ...

Statements by Israeli leaders to the effect that the destruction of civilian objects would be justified as a response to rocket attacks ("destroy 100 homes for every rocket fired") indicate the possibility of resorting to reprisals ... [which are] contrary to international humanitarian law. ...

Women and children especially affected

The military operations destroyed a substantial part of the economic infrastructure. As many factories were targeted and destroyed or damaged, poverty, unemployment and food insecurity further increased dramatically. The agricultural sector similarly suffered from the destruction of farmland, water wells and fishing boats during the military operations. ... The razing of farmland and the destruction of greenhouses are expected to further worsen food insecurity. ... Levels of stunting and thinness in children and of anemia prevalence in children and pregnant women were worrying even before the military operations. ...

The hardship caused by the extensive destruction of shelter (the United Nations Development Program reported 3,354 houses completely destroyed and 11,112 partially damaged) and the resulting displacement particularly affects children and women. ... Some 280 schools and kindergartens were destroyed. ...

Bombing meant to deny sustenance to the population

Israel has violated its obligation to allow free passage of all consignments of medical and hospital objects, food and clothing (article 23 of the Fourth Geneva Convention). ... Israel violated specific obligations which it has as the Occupying Power and which are spelled out in the Fourth Geneva Convention.

In the destruction by the Israeli armed forces of private residential houses, water wells, water tanks, agricultural land and greenhouses, there was a specific purpose of denying sustenance to the population of the Gaza Strip. The Mission finds that Israel violated its duty to respect the right of the Gaza population to an adequate standard of living, including access to adequate food, water and housing. The Mission, moreover, finds violations of specific human rights provisions protecting children, particularly those who are victims of armed conflict, women and the disabled.

The conditions of life in Gaza, resulting from deliberate actions of the Israeli armed forces and the declared policies of the Government of Israel—as they were presented by its authorized and legitimate representatives—with regard to the Gaza Strip before, during and after the military operation, cumulatively indicate the intention to inflict collective punishment on the people of the Gaza Strip in violation of international humanitarian law. ... The actions of the Government of Israel might justify a competent court finding that crimes against humanity have been committed. ...

Israel 'tightened hold on West Bank' during Gaza invasion

[The Mission found] a sharp rise in the use of force by the Israeli security forces against Palestinians in the West Bank from the beginning of the Israeli operations in Gaza. ... [D]uring the Israeli offensive in Gaza, restrictions on movement in the West Bank were tightened. ... There were more checkpoints in the West Bank, including in East Jerusalem, for the duration of the operation. ... During and following the operations in Gaza, Israel tightened its hold on the West Bank by increasing expropriations, house demolitions and demolition orders, granting more permits for homes built in settlements and intensifying the exploitation of the natural resources in the West Bank.

VIII

The People Break the Siege

In 2009, reflecting worldwide solidarity with the people of Gaza, many courageous grassroots organizations and individuals took it upon themselves to break the blockade of Gaza. They collected humanitarian aid and found ways to bring it to Gaza themselves. Among them was British Member of Parliament George Galloway, who that year organized three international Viva Palestina caravans, bringing to Gaza essential aid and as many international activists as possible, who then went back to their countries to report on what they had witnessed.

Every convoy had to struggle to get into Gaza. Covered here is the second Viva Palestina convoy, made entirely from people from the United States, which left New York City for Egypt via plane on July 4, 2009, and after overcoming many obstacles, made it into Gaza on July 15.

Viva Palestina caravan from U.S. enters Gaza.

Photo: www.vivapalestina-us.org

'We made it!'

Viva Palestina convoy delivers aid from U.S. people to Gaza

By John Parker
Published July 23, 2009

The largest U.S. humanitarian aid convoy to Palestine in history went over the Rafah border crossing into Gaza in the late evening of July 15, 2009. The 218-person contingent of activists brought more than $1 million in wheelchairs, walkers and medical supplies to the people of Gaza. The Egyptian government, however, limited the activists to only 24 hours in Gaza.

Sharon Eolis (left) and other delegates inside the Viva Palestina bus as it entered Gaza.

WW photo: John Parker

That the Viva Palestina caravan came from the U.S. is especially important, as Israel is the largest recipient of U.S. government aid in the world. Israel uses U.S. weapons and missiles against the Palestinian people on a daily basis.

Overcoming obstacles imposed by the U.S., Egyptian and Israeli regimes to lead the Viva Palestina group across the border were New York City Councilperson and lead negotiator for Viva Palestina-USA Charles Barron; former Congressperson Cynthia McKinney, just out of an Israeli prison for attempting to deliver aid by sea to Gaza with the Free Gaza Movement; and British MP George Galloway, who organized a caravan from Britain under the same name in March.

Charles Barron, Kevin Ovenden and Joy Nayo Simmons with boxes of medicine for humanitarian organizations.

Photo: John Parker

In spite of dishonest negotiations, arbitrary enforcement and ever-changing requirements for travel through Egypt to Gaza on the part of U.S. and Egyptian authorities, Viva Palestina was able to enter Gaza after making it through the Egyptian-enforced Israeli blockade. The challenges began on July 5 when the convoy arrived in Cairo.

Unified protests overcome challenges

Militant, unified protest actions met and overcame every challenge. The actions included letter-writing campaigns solicited instantly over the Internet and human chains surrounding buses at the Suez Canal. McKinney led a loud, impromptu protest session in Egyptian Customs.

When it appeared on July 13 that the Egyptian government was going to deny passage into Gaza, Viva Palestina supporters held emergency demonstrations at Egyptian consulates in New York, San Francisco, Houston, Chicago and other cities throughout the United States.

Egypt confiscates aid vehicles

One such hurdle, however, could not be overcome. The new vehicles purchased for medical agencies remain impounded by the Egyptian government in spite of the long back-and-forth sessions endured by the negotiating team. One of the seemingly final offers by the government of Egypt left vehicles impounded, no entrance into Gaza until most participants were scheduled to leave, and the stipulation that medical aid could be delivered only by the Israelis.

At a Viva Palestina meeting led by Barron in Cairo two days before the departure to Gaza, this option was presented for discussion with alternative offers to the government.

Galloway stated the desires of the inhabitants of Gaza, whose homes the Israelis destroyed and who have lost half of the hospitals with little access to basic necessities. They wanted the delegation's help in this order: first, convoy participants enter, then medical aid and finally the much-needed vehicles.

Neturei Karta anti-Zionist rabbis were part of the delegation and delivered aid.
Photo: John Parker

Why Gazans value convoy participants over aid

Why were the people in the contingent the most important for this effort in the eyes of the besieged people of Gaza? The mission had two goals. One was to provide medical supplies. The other was to expose the genocidal nature of this blockade and help create a political atmosphere that, if repeated enough, would chip away at the international silence and complicity in tolerating Israeli genocide.

All the aid in the world would be useless if Israel were allowed to stop its delivery. Putting pressure on people like President Barack Obama, who represents the country that holds the purse strings for Israel, is part of that political struggle.

The Viva Palestina-USA delegation, from the country Obama represents, entered Gaza with not only the medical aid, but with the determination to continue to increase exposure and visibility of this crisis and put one more nail in the coffin of Israeli occupation and genocide against the people of Palestine.

Among those participating in Viva Palestina-USA were representatives of the Council on American-Islamic Relations, Middle East Children's Alliance, Al Awda–the Palestine Right to Return Coalition, Cuba Coalition, Malcolm X Grassroots Movement, Movimiento Estudiantil Chicano de Aztlán (MEChA), American Muslims for Palestine, American Jewish Rabbis against Zionism, International Action Center, Answer Coalition, International Socialist Organization and Workers World Party.

For more on Viva Palestina efforts, visit www.vivapalestina-us.org.

Eyewitness Gaza:

'We saw destruction and courage'

Rafah, Gaza   WW photo: John Parker

By Sharon Eolis
Published July 31, 2009

We got in. We were in one of the last buses to arrive at the Gaza border in Rafah toward night in mid-July when Palestinian students greeted us and rode with us to Gaza City.

We soon entered Gaza City where a Palestinian delegation greeted us. They had waited all day and into the evening for all 218 Viva Palestina-U.S. members to arrive. We felt like we were entering free territory, where people were so warm and friendly to their guests and so glad to meet delegation members.

Huge holes in apartment building walls

The next morning we took a guided bus tour and witnessed Gaza's devastation. Apartment buildings had been shelled, leaving huge holes in the walls. Many homes in Gaza had been reduced to rubble.

We were told that thousands of homes were destroyed or made unlivable, leaving 50,000 Gaza Palestinians without shelter. The Israelis also bombed government buildings: the Parliament, the Cabinet building and the presidential compound.

There were gaping holes in the roofs and whole floors had been destroyed. One of the buildings had sheets of concrete hanging off it. In other places there were stacks of broken concrete and twisted metal.

'Factory row' destroyed

We passed an area known as Gaza's factory row. Before the bombing and invasion, more than 200 factories produced cement, biscuits, wooden furniture and much else. Some distance from the factory area were remnants of colorful carts from a demolished ice cream factory.

The Israeli attack destroyed all the main factories and the agricultural centers. We could see the damage to orchards and olive groves that had been bulldozed. As the bus approached the Mediterranean Sea, we saw part of the beach refugee camp of Gaza City, where some folks were living in tents while others were out in the open cooking food over fires under the hot sun.

Stench of raw sewage as pumping system destroyed

What was harder to see was the damage to the water and power infrastructure. The ongoing blockade directed at the elected Hamas government had reduced fuel entry to Gaza, which meant that power was cut to a few hours per day, stalling the water pumping system. After the December-January invasion, some 80 percent of the electrical system was out of service, disrupting service for major wells providing water access to 200,000 people.

Sewage has been a major problem in Gaza because of an inadequate pumping system and shortage of fuel, generators and spare parts. We passed areas where the stench of raw sewage was overwhelming. Our guide said that raw, untreated sewage is pumped directly into the sea.

Parts to repair water, power services blockaded

Palestinian technicians said returning water and power services to the 400,000 people without them could take only weeks, but could be done only if the Israelis allowed parts and equipment to enter Gaza. Israel has refused to allow any of the needed equipment across the checkpoint.

Like the 1990s U.S. blockade of Iraq, the Israeli blockade of Gaza keeps out chlorine used to make water safe to drink and to treat raw sewage. The Israeli excuse is that the chlorine may also be used for weapons. But the reality is that in Iraq thousands of children died from water-borne disease as a result of the prohibition against chlorine.

A number of buildings, including mosques, were spray-painted by the Israeli military with such racist hate slogans as "Hamas is dead" in Arabic and in English and "Arabs need to die," among others. Despite the slogans and despite the invasion, Hamas still governs Gaza and the Palestinian resistance continues.

Refugee family driven from Be'ersheba

Jehad Abu-Jakar, a student at the University of Gaza studying English, told us how hard it was to study in Gaza. The university lacks books, school supplies, and vehicles and fuel for transportation. Recently he moved from his home on the Rafah border, only 300 yards from the Egyptian checkpoint where the convoy entered Gaza, to Gaza City so he can continue his studies.

Abu-Jakar explained how the Israelis forced his family out of Bir al-Saba (Be'ersheba) in 1948 and how they came to the Gaza Strip as refugees, where they had hoped to build a better life. His childhood on the border during the first Intifada was very difficult.

During the second Intifada the Israelis killed Abu-Jakar's aunt and injured his mother. At that time he joined with other youth and threw stones at the Israeli forces. His story of the human devastation and suffering of one family reflects the conditions for many Palestinian families who live on the Gaza Strip, where invasions, destruction and brutality have continued for more than 60 years.

The people of Gaza are continuing their struggle and resistance against the months-long blockade and Israeli incursions and attacks.

Medical supplies almost nonexistent

Gaza health services were on the brink of collapse before the Dec. 27, 2008, Israeli invasion. Medical supplies were almost nonexistent, and patients with complex medical conditions were being referred to hospitals outside Gaza.

Aed Yohi, a representative of the Palestinian Medical Relief Society, said at a press conference that Gaza has a total of 2,053 hospital beds.

The invasion killed more than 1,400 Palestinians, including more than 300 children, while 13 Israelis died, 4 of them from "friendly fire." About a quarter of the Palestinian casualties occurred by Dec. 30, 2008. At that time only 15 medical patients were allowed to pass through the

Rafah border into Egypt for emergency care, according to the World Health Organization.

An article on the Web site Mideastcurrent.com from that time illustrates how the blockade affected medical care during the invasion. At Al Shifa' hospital on Dec. 30, 2008, Khaled Abu-Najar, a staff nurse in the emergency department, said that "150 patients were brought in at once ... [but] we lacked beds, sterile gloves, gauze, sheets and scissors to treat patients."

'No artery clamps, chest tubes to treat severe trauma'

At the same hospital, Ramez Zyam, one of the general surgeons who was working 24-hour shifts, said the surgeons treating many crush injuries and severe trauma lacked instruments like artery clamps, chest tubes and forceps needed to handle severe traumatic injuries. They had not received medical supplies for three months. According to the director of the hospital, Hussein Ashur, the burn, intensive care, orthopedic and surgery units reached capacity.

The Kamal Adwan Hospital serves Jabalya and Beit Lahlya. Jabalya is Gaza's largest refugee camp and 300,000 people reside there. This hospital has only 71 beds. The first day of the invasion they received 93 patients for emergency care. This hospital lacked supplies, ambulances and staff. But they expanded makeshift beds and continued to care for the wounded.

Supplies still needed

The need for medical supplies continues even without a war emergency. Our convoy brought a number of truckloads of medical supplies with us from the U.S., including walkers, wheelchairs, crutches and other disability-assistance equipment to help the people wounded during the invasion. The convoy brought medicine and other medical supplies, like intensive care monitors, purchased in the U.S. and materials bought in Egypt. Much of it was aimed at aiding people who had lost limbs.

Egypt stops Palestinian convoy volunteer from bringing his family out of Gaza

At the end of our 24 hours allowed by Egypt in Gaza, we had a wrenching confirmation that no one can officially get in or out of Gaza unless given permission at border checkpoints, which are opened at the whim of Israel and Egypt. If your name is not on a pre-existing list, you can't get into Gaza or leave it.

A Palestinian man with a U.S. passport, who was part of the Viva Palestina convoy, tried to bring his family out of Gaza so they could travel back to the U.S. Although his spouse and children have U.S. passports, Egyptian border guards refused to allow the bus through the checkpoint with them aboard.

Convoy delegates tried to carry the children across the border, but security guards refused to allow this and held the bus up for over an hour. Only those who had been on the bus when it entered Gaza were allowed to return. The Palestinian delegate had to leave his family behind when he returned to Egypt.

The task ahead for convoy members is to spread the word about Gaza and our experiences there with pictures, videos, newspaper articles and presentations to groups around the United States to win more support for the Palestinian struggle on the Gaza Strip and for their heroic resistance against Israel and U.S. imperialism.

The 218 participants in Viva Palestina-U.S. will be taking on that task.

Seeing Israel's prisons through Palestinian eyes

"The ICRC Family Visits Program in the Gaza Strip was suspended in 2007, barring all means of communication between Gazan prisoners and the outside world."
　　　—Goldstone Report

By Sharon Eolis
Gaza City
Published Aug. 27, 2009

Many of the statistics here are from the blog of the International Campaign of Solidarity with the Palestinian Prisoners.

More than 11,000 Palestinian women, men and children are incarcerated in Israeli maximum security facilities like Nufha, Haderim, Jalamy, and Ashkalon, among others.

In Gaza City, a group of Palestinian women with family members languishing in Israeli prisons described for convoy visitors the horrific conditions in these concentration camps.

Mothers in Gaza show pictures of their imprisoned sons.

WW photo: Judy Greenspan

Muhammad Hassamand, the spouse of one of the women, has spent 23 years in prison. His sons, one 12 and another 15, cannot see their father. His spouse said, "We didn't go to them. The Israelis came to our land. We are the indigenous people. There are more than 11,000 Palestinians in Israeli jails [compared to] one Israeli soldier," being held in Gaza.

Another elderly woman told of losing her eyesight after her son went to prison. "I lost my eyes from crying all day and night for my son. My son has been sentenced for the rest of his life. He has spent more than 20 years in prison. For more than 10 years, I didn't see him in my eyes, and now I can't. I want to see my son. We want our efforts and your efforts to help release him."

Never allowed to visit husband jailed for 22 years

Another woman said, "My husband has been held in an Israeli prison for 22 years, and I have never been allowed to visit." She thinks her son is also incarcerated in Israel, but she doesn't know if he is alive or dead.

Since 1967, over 700,000 Palestinians—20 percent of the total population in the occupied territories—have been arrested. The vast majority are men—approximately 40 percent of the total male Palestinian population.

Since the second Intifada began in 2000, more than 70,000 Palestinians, including at least 850 women, have been arrested by Israel, according to Abdullah al-Zeghari, director of the Bethlehem branch of the Palestinian Prisoners' Society.

Many believe that imprisonment and torture are a core element of the Israeli occupation's strategy of collective containment and punishment of the Palestinian people.

Anyone who the Israelis think will resist the occupation is in danger of being imprisoned. This includes nonmilitary political activists, community organizers, paramedics, doctors, journalists, teachers and students as well as resistance fighters.

'85 percent of prisoners are tortured'

According to the Israeli Information Center for Human Rights in the Occupied Territories, B'Tselem, more than 85 percent of Palestinians detained since 1967 have been subjected to torture, and at least 197 have died in prison. Medical negligence was the cause of 50 deaths. The rest were from torture or executions.

Until 1999 nearly all Palestinian prisoners were tortured for information based on the Landau Ministerial Committee (1987) policy that allowed "moderate physical and psychological pressure." This was after an Israeli High Court of Justice ruling prohibited the use of several forms of torture.

Treatment like U.S. jails at Abu Ghraib, Guantanamo

The police and army, however, continue to use prohibited methods, similar to the treatment prisoners have been subjected to at Abu Ghraib in Iraq and Guantánamo Bay prison.

Forms of torture used include beatings, kicking, strip searches, sleep deprivation, verbal abuse and psychological threats, including those against family members. Prisoners have been bound to chairs in painful positions or forced to crouch in a frog-like position.

Prisoners have been kept in solitary confinement or held in tents in the desert in extreme temperatures. Prisoners' food has been placed next to the holes used as toilets. Inmates have been denied access to hot water or change of clothing.

All these conditions are against United Nations' basic human rights standards.

Medical negligence: care, medicines withheld

More than 1,600 prisoners suffer from chronic diseases but are denied care. The prison administration refuses to give permission for surgery for such life-threatening conditions as cancers or for kidney transplants. It also refuses to allow into the jails medicine from families, physicians or the Red Cross.

Administrative detention, where a person can be held for extended periods of time with no trial or formal charges, is a violation of international and human rights law, particularly the Fourth Geneva Convention.

Administrative detention in Israel was originally based on the British Mandate Defense (Emergency) Regulation of 1945. It allowed police to hold a prisoner based on confidential information that the detainee and her/his lawyer are not allowed to see. While a detainee is allowed an appeal, the confidential nature of the "evidence" makes a fair trial impossible.

This practice is still in effect in Israel. According to Israel Prisons Service (IPS), as of May 31, 2009, there were at least 449 Palestinian administrative detainees. This number was as high as 849 in November

2007. Palestinian detainees have been held under administrative detention orders from six months to eight years.

Pregnant women must deliver in cells

Presently 63 women political prisoners are held in Hasharon and Damoon prisons. Some are as young as 14. They are subjected to humiliating treatment, including strip searches, sometimes in the presence of men.

Pregnant women are forced to deliver their babies in prison cells where these infants continue to live with their mothers for years. Since 1967 the Israeli army has captured more than 10,000 Palestinian women. Eight hundred were kidnapped during the al-Aqsa Intifada in September 2000.

The Israeli Defense Forces have kidnapped a total of 7,600 children, male and female, since 2000. Some were as young as 12 years old. According to IPS February 2009 reports, there were 374 Palestinian children in jail; 50 were under 16 years old.

The Israeli army considers children age 16 to be adults. This is in violation of the U.N. Convention on the Rights of the Child, to which Israel is a signer.

Child prisoners denied family visits, education

These children are also subjected to torture and forced confession. Many are held in jails with adult prisoners and subjected to sexual and physical violence. They may be denied family visits, deprived of medical care, and suffer from theft of personal belongings. They are also deprived of education, recreation facilities and culture, and are tortured during attempts to coerce them to collaborate with Israel.

Like prisoners in the U.S. (the majority of whom are Black and Latino/a), most incarcerated Palestinians are held in jails far from their homes. Since Hamas was elected in 2006, Israel has outlawed family visits to prisoners.

New ruling allows arrest with no evidence

Also like the U.S., Israel has enacted a new status called "unlawful combatant." This legalizes the detention of Lebanese and Arab prisoners even when there is no evidence for trial. This law is now applied to the people of Gaza.

Palestinians in Gaza hold one Israeli soldier prisoner, Gilad Shalit, captured in 2006. They have offered to exchange Shalit for those held by

Israel. While using this prisoner as an excuse for its wars on the people of Gaza, Israel has refused to negotiate any prisoner exchange

Palestinian prisoners have a long history of resistance in Israeli jails. They have organized hunger strikes to protest violent attacks on prisoners and denial of visits and medical care. In some cases thousands of prisoners have participated. The Israeli police and security forces have responded with great brutality.

The prisoners demonstrated their solidarity during the July 2006 war on Lebanon and during the Israeli war and massacre in Gaza that began in December 2008.

The Palestinian people are requesting that the international community call protests and launch long-term campaigns to end the incarceration of Palestinians in Israeli prisons as part of full liberation for the people of Palestine.

Report to Black community:
Their children also ask, 'Why do they hate us?'

By Dolores Cox
Brooklyn, N.Y.
Published Aug. 8, 2009

On July 29, 2009, the House of the Lord Church in Brooklyn hosted a standing-room-only report-back meeting led by several participants of the Viva Palestina historic U.S. convoy who returned on July 17 and 18, 2009, from Gaza City in Palestine. The multinational audience was majority Black.

New York City Councilperson Charles Barron and two of his staff members participated in the Gaza convoy. Barron spoke about the racial, religious and cultural diversity of the convoy, including youths who are Hip-Hop artists.

Barron—an African American who refers to himself as an elected revolutionary, not an elected politician—commented that he went to Gaza because "the struggle of the Palestinians is the struggle of all oppressed people of color in the U.S., Africa, Latin America and elsewhere; that we all share the same oppressor, the same enemy— vicious U.S. and European white supremacists; that the oppressor is determined to oppress by any means necessary."

Barron compared the children of Gaza to children in the U.S., saying, "They have no childhood." Israel destroyed their schools, playgrounds, toys and homes. In addition, many children are dying of starvation, forced upon them by Israel's siege and blockade. The bombing and invasion of Gaza have left them traumatized.

A video was shown during the meeting that illustrated the stark reality of the destruction in Gaza. The convoy's minibuses displayed Palestinian and U.S. flags. African Americans carried the red, black and green African Liberation flag—red for bloodshed, black for the people, green for the land—it was explained. Palestinians were visibly touched by this support. Barron said, "Iraq has been occupied since 2003; Palestine has been occupied for 60 years."

One section of the video labeled "Brave little girls" showed children speaking about their experiences. The children asked the same perennial questions that millions of Black children in the U.S. and throughout the African Diaspora ask who have been targeted by white supremacists: "Why do they hate us so much? What did we ever do to them?"

IX

Egypt Enforces Israeli Blockade

It is generally believed that Israel is on one side and the Arabs are on the other. But this view, often seen in the establishment media, does not consider that all nations have different classes, and different class points of view. For example, on key questions the Arab regimes and the Arab people often stand at opposite poles. Take the Palestine question. Reactionary Arab regimes quietly support Israel and oppose freedom for Palestine, while the Arab people overwhelmingly oppose Israeli aggression and passionately support Palestinian rights.

The first article in this chapter, describing Egyptian repression of the third Viva Palestina convoy, illustrates just how much the Mubarak regime in Egypt is an active party to the Israeli siege and blockade of Gaza. The second article, an interview with Palestinian Marxist Dr. Adel Samara, explains why.

Despite outpouring of solidarity in eight countries

2,000 Egypt police attack and beat volunteers in third Viva Palestina convoy

By Bill Doares
Published Jan. 15, 2010

For the third time in a year, Viva Palestina, the international relief effort led by British Member of Parliament George Galloway, has broken the siege of Gaza.

On Jan. 6, 2010, some 518 volunteers from many countries drove more than 156 vehicles loaded with tons of medicine and other humanitarian aid into Gaza, the only part of Palestine independent of Israeli control. They were backed by a global outpouring of solidarity, especially from the people of Turkey and the Arab and Islamic world, and as far away as Malaysia.

When the convoy entered Gaza after its month-long, 5,000-mile journey, hundreds of thousands of Gaza's 1.5 million people lined the streets in welcome. "The sight of peo-

Jan. 6, 2010, New York demonstration hails Viva Palestina's convoy to Gaza.
WW photo: John Catalinotto

ple lining the streets virtually the full length of the Gaza Strip, after waiting for 10 hours for our last vehicles to pass (thanks to further Egyptian delays), was the only vindication that this initiative ever required," said convoy leader Kevin Ovenden.

Egyptian troops fire across border on people in Gaza

The third "Lifeline to Gaza" convoy defied an international conspiracy against the people of Gaza by the military/banker regime in Washington, D.C.; the U.S.-funded Israeli apartheid state; and the U.S.-funded Mubarak dictatorship in Egypt.

The day before they entered Gaza, the international volunteers were assaulted and beaten by 2,000 Egyptian riot police and undercover cops with clubs, stones and water cannons. Fifty-five people were injured, some seriously, and seven arrested. Egyptian troops opened fire across the border on people in Gaza itself who were protesting the attack on the convoy. Israeli missiles also struck Gaza while the convoy was there, killing three Palestinians.

Convoy leader seized and deported from Egypt

After returning from Gaza, MP Galloway was seized by undercover cops, forced on a plane to London and barred from returning to Egypt.

Lifeline Three left London on Dec. 6, 2009, with 200 volunteers and 80 trucks and ambulances filled with supplies donated by people across Britain and Ireland. It drove through Europe, warmly welcomed and joined by people, trucks and supplies in Belgium, Italy and Greece. A huge popular outpouring greeted the convoy in Turkey, where 125 people, including 10 MPs, and 60 more vehicles joined the convoy.

Massive crowd greets aid convoy in Turkey

International Action Center activist Ralph Loeffler, one of 62 U.S. volunteers on the journey, reported: "For the first time in 30 years the Turkish government permitted a political demonstration in historic Taksim Square, and it was to support Viva Palestina's medical relief convoy to blockaded Gaza. A massive, enthusiastic crowd turned out in the pouring winter rain to hear George Galloway and Kevin Ovenden thank the Turkish people and government for supporting Viva Palestina's third convoy to Gaza.

"After leaving Taksim the convoy proceeded to Adapazari [Turkey] to overnight in a sports stadium. Although the convoy arrived about 2 a.m., the citizens of Adapazari were there and ready to help. Locals swarmed the vehicles and buses to carry ... the 200 convoy participants' sleeping gear and baggage into the stadium."

In Syria, a British volunteer reported, "We were greeted by the sound of music and cheering. At the border posts, a huge reception was waiting for us, with speeches, music, flowers and flag-waving customs officers.

"There were also many, many Palestinians from the Syrian refugee camps, whose welcome was overwhelming. They told us we were heroes, angels, and thanked us over and over again for helping Gaza. We could only tell them that it was our duty, our obligation, and an honor to do what we can to fight the occupation — what else can you say when you experience such hospitality from people who've been exiled from their homeland for more than 60 years? It was a humbling experience. ...

Palestinian girl: 'You give us strength to carry on'

"One 12-year-old girl said to this reporter: 'I'd like to come with you to my country, to see my land, but I'm not allowed. Thank you for going. It gives us the strength to carry on.'"

In Jordan, too, the convoy was officially welcomed by the government and warmly welcomed by the people. But when they reached the Red Sea port of Aqaba, Jordan, whence they had planned to take a ferry to Egypt's Sinai Peninsula and drive to Gaza, the Mubarak regime told them they could only enter Egypt through the Mediterranean port of Al-Arish. This forced the convoy's return to Syria, from whence a Turkish ship conveyed the vehicles to Egypt while the majority of volunteers followed by plane.

Egyptian people support convoy, oppose regime

The Egyptian regime's open subservience to the Israeli state — which has twice invaded Egypt (in 1956 and 1967), murdered thousands of Egyptians, including schoolchildren and prisoners of war, and executed hundreds of Egyptian prisoners in cold blood — shocked even veteran political activists. It is in stark contrast to the attitude of ordinary Egyptians, who at every opportunity have expressed sympathy with the Viva Palestina convoys.

When the first 167 VP participants landed at Al-Arish, Egyptian authorities seized their passports and told them the rest of the convoy would not be allowed in. After a sit-in at the airport, Egyptian authorities backed down temporarily, but the next day told the convoy leaders that 43 of the vehicles and their contents would have to pass through Israeli-controlled territory.

Standoff when Egypt tries to seize aid trucks

When Viva Palestina leaders tried to negotiate that demand, pointing out the aid would be unlikely to reach Gaza, the Mubarak regime sent in police to try and seize the trucks. Plainclothes cops hurled rocks at the volunteers while uniformed police attacked with clubs, gas and water cannons. The activists stood up to the assault, however, even capturing one of the assailants, and a standoff ensued. Viva Palestina agreed to the Egyptian regime's demand in return for the release of convoy members arrested by Egyptian authorities. The supplies the

Egyptians did not allow in will be sent to Turkey and distributed there to people in need.

The violence against Viva Palestina came only a week after Mubarak's police attacked the 1,400-strong Gaza Freedom March and prevented it from bringing aid to Gaza. The regime took a very different attitude toward Israeli Prime Minister Benjamin Netanyahu, who received a warm welcome in Cairo on the anniversary of Israel's assault on Gaza. In the 1970s Netanyahu was involved in terrorist operations in Egypt as part of the Zionist special operations unit Sayeret Matkal.

Viva Palestina's third entry into Gaza was a people's victory in spite of the force arrayed against it. It not only brought in much-needed aid, but it posed a powerful political challenge to the blockade. Said Ovenden: "We launched Viva Palestina with a strategic outlook that we could crack open the siege by fusing aid, a savvy understanding of the political context and campaigning. We think this effort is working and can contribute to the growing international movement in solidarity with the Palestinian people."

U.S. funds Mubarak to block Gaza's supply tunnels

While solidarity with the besieged Palestinians of Gaza is growing, so is their peril. With U.S. funds and help from the U.S. Army Corps of Engineers, the Mubarak regime is building an 80-foot-deep wall along Gaza's southern border to block the tunnels that are Gaza's primary lifeline. And there is growing evidence Israel is preparing another full-scale assault on Gaza.

The lengths to which the forces of oppression are going in order to crush the people of Gaza make it incumbent on the people's movement to redouble efforts to break the blockade. The Viva Palestina movement appears determined to rise to the call. Upon his return to London, George Galloway told the media: "I've been banned from returning to Egypt, but that doesn't mean I'm not going back to Gaza. There's more than one way into Gaza."

Videos and first-hand accounts of the convoy may be found at vivapalestina.org.

Why Arab reactionary regimes like Egypt do imperialism's bidding

WW interviews Palestinian Marxist Dr. Adel Samara

By Joyce Chediac
Published Jan. 10, 2010

The corporate media have much to say about the Arab countries and developments in the Middle East. Rarely, however, do these media permit people from the Middle Eastern countries to speak for themselves.

Dr. Adel Samara is a Palestinian Marxist from the West Bank city of Ramallah. Dr. Samara is the author of more than 15 books on the relationship of forces in the Middle East, and editor-in-chief of *Kana'an,* a quarterly magazine (kanaanonline.org). His views are very different from the views covered in the *New York Times* or Fox TV.

Arab comprador regimes created by imperialism

Asked why the Egyptian government is aiding Israel and the U.S. in the siege and blockade of Gaza, Samara gave a history of how most Arab regimes were actually set up by imperialist powers to be their dependents and agents of reaction in the Middle East.

The 1916 Sykes-Picot Treaty between Britain, France and Russia, he said, "divided up the area, fragmenting it into small countries and put a king in every place. Weak and poor aristocratic elements" agreed to be financed by imperialism. "These rulers were unable to last

Dr. Adel Samara

WW photo

without support of the imperialists. And they competed among themselves."

This has led to a situation where "the imperialist powers, especially the U.S., pretend democracy while supporting the worst regimes in the history of the Arab nation." This is an attempt "to prove there is no Arab nationality — this regime fights that one — ... and because the imperialists know that an increase in Arab unity won't be good for Israel."

Samara explained that from the time that the World Zionist Organization began meeting in 1897, and when Britain backed a Zionist state in 1917 with the Balfour Declaration, it was clear the Zionists had plans for a pro-imperialist state in Palestine. Yet, "In 1948 and earlier, Arab regimes allowed Jews from Arab countries to go to Palestine. Arab regimes knew that Jews would be soldiers for a Jewish state in Palestine. Arab regimes contributed [to this state]."

Arab armies that fought for Palestine in 1948 staged revolts later

It is well known that in the 1948 war and campaign of Zionist-imperialist terrorism that erased Palestine from the map and replaced it with Israel, the Arab armies were defeated. Not so well known is the fact that "the 1948 Arab armies together were smaller than the Zionist army. The Arab regimes did not take defending Palestine seriously."

There were exceptions. "In 1948, Iraqi military forces fought the hardest and were in a strategic position on what became the 1948 dividing line. But they were forced to withdraw. As a result, the Iraqi regime lost credibility. ... Some of these Iraqi military leaders forced by their government to retreat from defending Palestine in 1948 took part in the 1958 revolution in Iraq," which deposed a pro-British monarch.

Another exception occurred in the Egyptian army. "In 1948, Gamal Abdel Nasser, then an officer in the Egyptian army, was in Fallujah [Iraq]. He and other leaders of the Egyptian army refused to give up, and were under siege for several months." The refusal of the Egyptian regime of King Farouk to back Nasser and his soldiers "created a bitterness between the Egyptian masses and the leadership. It is why, in 1952, the people supported the coup" of the young officers' movement, headed by Nasser, which toppled King Farouk.

"From 1948 to 1966 Jews living in the Arab countries, Arab Jews, were allowed to go to Palestine, especially from Morocco and Iraq. In Iraq, from 1948 to 1958, the prime minister's son was the owner of the Iraqi airline and airlifted [Iraqi Jews] to Palestine. The Arab regimes gave the Israeli regime cheap labor to be exploited by Ashkenazi," that is, Jewish people from Europe from whom Israel's ruling class was formed.

1967 war on Palestinians also aimed at progressive Nasser government in Egypt

Israel started the 1967 war, attacking Jordan, Egypt and Syria and seizing and occupying the West Bank, Gaza and Sinai. "The main goal in 1967 was to destroy the Nasserist regime in Egypt." This was because "in 1963, when a progressive current took power in Yemen and Saudi Arabia interfered, the Egyptian army went to Yemen to support the new government." The West was concerned that oil-rich Saudi Arabia could be hit from Yemen.

"In 1967, the defeated Arab comprador regimes left the battle. From 1967 to 1973, most Arab regimes stopped contributing to the Palestine struggle."

Cairo action Dec. 28, 2008, in solidarity with Gaza. The Egyptian people are against their government's enforcement of the blockade.

From 1965 to 1970 Palestinians initiated their own struggles, independently of the Arab comprador regimes. Dr. Samara said, "The Arab regimes tried to contain this struggle, mainly by giving money to the rightwing [of the PLO] headed by Yasser Arafat, which became very rich. This containment continues today. The role of the Arab regimes is to contain, interfere with and destroy the Palestinian movement. This is one of the main reasons why a united Palestinian front never developed within the Palestine Liberation Organization."

Sadat sides Egypt with Israel against Palestinians

"The Arab regimes continued this policy," he added. Anwar Sadat, who became the Egyptian head of state after Nasser's death, turned his country again towards imperialism after first winning popular credibility by retaking the Suez Canal in 1973. In 1978, Sadat entered negotiations with Israeli Prime Minister Menachem Begin at Camp David and declared he would visit Israel. Sadat went along with Begin, who said, "What we will give the Palestinians is only autonomy and not a state."

Dr. Samara pointed out that in 1970, in what became known as the Black September assault, King Hussein of Jordan attacked the Palestinian presence in Jordan, killing thousands and forcing the Palestinian Resistance into Lebanon.

And when Israel attacked Lebanon in 2006, he said, "Egypt, Saudi Arabia and Jordan encouraged Israel to destroy Hezbollah." But this attack failed in the face of determined Hezbollah resistance.

Now, "Egypt is enforcing the siege on Gaza — where there is not enough food, no access to health care or other key supplies."

The current Arab comprador regimes are "against resistance. They are in the camp of the enemy and against peace for the Palestinian people. ... A change is needed in the Arab homeland" away from "the leaders who opened it up for all foreign powers."

Nationalism of the comprador class vs. the nationalism of the workers

"Under direct and indirect colonialism there is an unequal exchange. Nationalism is an important tool in grouping people for developing cooperation and unity, especially in the Third World."

But there is also a class divide, Dr. Samara said. "The nationalism of the comprador is dependent and selfish — only for the sake of the ruling class. It is tied to imperialism.

"The nationalism of the bourgeoisie is against socialism. ... The nationalism of the working class is nationalism open to socialism because this class has an interest in socialism."

X

Piracy at Sea: Gaza Freedom Flotilla Attacked by Israel

The Gaza Freedom Flotilla consisted of six ships carrying 750 people and food, medicine and housing materials for Gaza. Starting out in Turkey, the ships were crossing the Mediterranean Sea to break the blockade of Gaza and deliver the aid. On May 31, 2010, while the ships were in international waters, the Israeli military surrounded the flotilla and staged a commando raid on the flotilla's largest ship, the Mavi Marmara, killing nine people aboard and wounding dozens more.

Nine killed as 'Troops started firing before they even touched down'

By LeiLani Dowell
Published June 2, 2010

A firestorm of condemnation and protest has followed Israel's latest brutality—the massacre of nine unarmed activists by the Israeli navy in international waters north of Gaza. The activists were part of a 750-member delegation on a six-boat flotilla attempting to bring humanitarian aid to the besieged people of Gaza.

The Freedom Flotilla was the largest attempt to date in the growing movement to break a three-year blockade of Gaza by Israel. Led by the Free Gaza Movement and Insani Yardim Vakfi, a Turkish organization, the flotilla carried some 10,000 tons of humanitarian aid, including medical and construction supplies.

New York demonstration protesting the flotilla killings.   WW photo: G. Dunkel

Representing 40 different countries, participants in the international delegation included 85-year-old Holocaust survivor Hedy Epstein and government diplomats from various countries.

Unwarranted attack in international waters

Some 70 miles off the Israeli coast, Israeli naval vessels and a helicopter surrounded the convoy on May 31, 2010. In an act of piracy, heavily masked Israeli commandoes slid down ropes from helicopters onto the largest of the six convoy ships, the Mavi Marmara. Journalists aboard the ship reported that the troops started firing before they even touched down. Reports also note that passengers aboard the ship were waving white flags at the time of the invasion.

'We communicated that we were unarmed'

Huwaida Arraf, a Free Gaza Movement leader, told the *New York Times*: "We communicated to [the Israeli Defense Forces] clearly that we are unarmed civilians. We asked them not to use violence."

Houston protest after the attack on the Mavi Marmara.

In an absurd propaganda spin, the Israeli Defense Forces claimed that upon boarding the ship, the IDF naval soldiers were met with "live fire and weaponry including knives and clubs," forcing them to use what they called "riot dispersal means." Suggesting that the activists did not have the right to defend themselves against the attack, the military reports the wounding of four Israeli soldiers as justification for the slaying of innocent civilians aboard the ship. Danny Ayalon, Israeli deputy foreign minister, also claimed at a press conference that "the organizers are well known for their ties to global jihad, Al Qaeda and Hamas."

According to reports, the Israeli navy seized all six ships and, after telling the press the ships would be taken to Ashdod, towed them to Haifa to avoid scrutiny. Meanwhile, all other participants aboard the ships have been imprisoned or deported.

Worldwide protests condemn massacre

Protests broke out around the world in condemnation of the massacre. Massive rallies took place in Turkey, where protesters attempted to storm the Israeli Consulate in Istanbul. Demonstrations were held in Cyprus, Iraq, Norway, Sweden and in Paris, Rome and more than 20 cities in Greece.

In the U.S. emergency protests were held May 31, 2010, in cities throughout the country in spite of the Memorial Day holiday. Protesters denounced the U.S. for providing military and other material support to client-state Israel, allowing it to carry out such atrocities. The Obama administration has pledged at least $30 billion in military aid to Israel over the next 10 years.

Turkey recalls ambassador, charges 'state terrorism'

Turkey's government, which had in large part sponsored the flotilla, immediately recalled its ambassador from Israel and requested an emergency meeting of the U.N. Security Council that was held on May 31, 2010. Turkey's Prime Minister Recep Tayyip Erdogan called the incident "state terrorism."

Other governments were forced to respond as well. Both Turkey and Greece canceled joint military exercises they had planned with Israel, and Israeli envoys were summoned by the governments of Turkey, Egypt, Jordan and several European countries in protest of the attack.

Murat Mercan, the head of the Turkish Grand National Assembly's foreign affairs commission, noted on television: "We are going to see in the following days whether Israel has done it as a display of decisiveness or to commit political suicide." (*New York Times*, May 31, 2010)

Obama does not condemn attack

The response from the U.S. was far milder. After a June 1, 2010, meeting in Washington between President Barack Obama and Israeli Prime Minister Benjamin Netanyahu was canceled, the *New York Times* reported that rather than expressing condemnation of the raid, the White House "released a statement saying that President Obama had spoken with Mr. Netanyahu and understood his need to return immediately to Israel. In addition to regrets about the loss of life, 'the president also expressed the importance of learning all the facts and circumstances around this morning's tragic events as soon as possible,' the statement said." (May 31, 2010)

Siege leaves Gazans impoverished, with health deteriorating

A recent World Health Organization (WHO) report states that the health of Gaza's population continues to deteriorate as a result of the Israeli blockade—a form of collective punishment unleashed by Israel after Hamas took electoral power in the area.

The WHO report notes acute shortages of cooking gas, fuel and other basic necessities in Gaza and states that 98 percent of industrial operations have been shut down since 2007. A ban on the import of building materials means that some 6,400 homes destroyed by Israel's 2008-2009 bombings have not been rebuilt. The same military operation destroyed water and sanitation infrastructure that Gazans have also been unable to repair, according to a May 18 IRIN report. (IRIN, the Integrated Regional Information Network, is a news agency that focuses on human rights issues in regions often neglected by establishment media.)

The report shows 56 percent of Gazans living below the poverty level in the third quarter of 2008, with chronic malnutrition at 10.2 percent. However, the situation is not much better for the rest of Palestine, with 51 percent of all Palestinians living below the poverty level in the same period.

Steadfastness of Palestinians inspires people's movement

The continued attacks on the Palestinian people and their steadfast allies will only increase the call for boycott, divestment and sanctions against Israel. This most recent atrocity exposes not only the ruthlessness of the settler Israeli state—and the U.S. as its sponsor—but also shows the steadfastness and determination of people around the world to free Palestine.

Gaza Freedom Flotilla—
The new Freedom Riders

By Joyce Chediac
Published June 16, 2010

The heroes and heroines of the Gaza Freedom Flotilla, so brutally attacked by Israeli commandos on May 31, 2010, have transformed the struggle to break the siege of Gaza and raised it to a higher level. They are the new Freedom Riders.

Freedom Riders were civil rights activists who rode interstate buses into the southern United States 50 years ago to defy racist segregation practices. Like the Palestinians, the African-American population of the South lived under a separate, apartheid system, called "Jim Crow."

Merely because these Black and white activists traveled together, ate together and shared facilities together where it was forbidden, they were attacked, beaten and even murdered by racists. Their vehicles were firebombed while the local police looked away. Their willingness to risk their lives exposed the

Freedom Riders with a burning bus at Anniston, Ala., May 1961.

brutality of Jim Crow racism and inspired others, who were appalled by the violence against them.

Freedom Riders transformed the civil rights movement and marked a turning point in that struggle, which then grew throughout the South.

When nine courageous Gaza Freedom Flotilla activists were killed and scores wounded by Israeli commandos on May 31, 2010, for merely trying to bring food, medicine and housing materials to the besieged people of Gaza, the world

Freedom Riders challenge segregation of interstate travel, 1960.

was horrified and outraged. The illusion that Israel had any legitimate case against the people or government of Gaza was shattered and Israeli brutality exposed before the world.

More Freedom Flotillas are now on their way to Gaza, and the worldwide Boycott, Divestment and Sanctions campaign against Israel is growing by leaps and bounds.

Israeli investigation called 'farce'

Rejecting a United Nations call for an international inquiry into its murderous commando raid, on June 14, 2010, Israel's Cabinet approved an Israeli government-appointed commission to investigate its own attack on the aid ship. This "independent public commission" isn't really independent. Led by retired Israeli Supreme Court Justice Jacob Turkel, it will have two foreign observers, but only as non-voting members.

Israel claims its commission would "examine the legality of Israel's naval blockade of Gaza and whether the raid on the flotilla conformed with the rules of international law." (*New York Times*, June 14, 2010)

But *Ha'aretz*, Israel's newspaper of record, says that the Israeli government really seeks to investigate its victims. "The truth that Netanyahu wishes to bring out involves the identity of the flotilla's organizers, its sources of funding, and the knives and rods that were brought aboard," the paper wrote. "He does not intend to probe the decision-making process that preceded the takeover of the ship and the shortcomings that were uncovered." (*Ha'aretz*, June 13, 2010)

Even *Ha'aretz* calls this investigation a "farce."

U.S.: A silent partner in Israeli commando raid

Washington, it seems, is a participant in the farce. Just hours after Israel announced its "independent" investigation, White House spokesperson Robert Gibbs "welcomed" it as "an important step forward."

Washington has criticized neither Israel's commando attack nor its 36-month blockade of Gaza. U.S. officials have said as little as possible about the commando raid, while continuing to funnel funds to Tel Aviv. In fact, Washington's huge economic and military support for Israel and its political cover for Tel Aviv make it accountable for Israeli actions and a silent partner in the deadly commando raid.

While Washington may disagree with Israeli tactics, the Pentagon has its hands full with the wars in Afghanistan and Iraq. Israel remains the Pentagon's most reliable ally to keep the oppressed Palestinians and other peoples in line in that oil-rich and strategic area. There are no splits on this in U.S. ruling circles.

Recently Congress added $205 million to the $3 billion the U.S. already gives the Israeli military each year for a missile system. The additional sum was approved by a bipartisan vote of 401 legislators.

Flotilla forces Egypt, Arab League response

In addition to changing the character of the struggle, the Freedom Flotilla is responsible for a chain of political events. On June 7, 2010, an Egyptian security official declared the blockade on Gaza a "failure" and opened Egypt's border with Gaza "indefinitely."

Egypt is one of the most repressive regimes in the area and has collaborated with Israel in the siege of Gaza. Egypt had previously placed every obstacle in the way of Viva Palestina delegations attempting to deliver humanitarian aid to Gaza via Egypt's border. This included physically attacking the delegations, threatening to strand them in the Sinai Desert, confiscating their material aid and deporting their leaders.

Egypt has now opened the Gaza border out of fear of its own population, which has been inspired by the solidarity of the Freedom Flotilla and angered by the Israeli attack. This opening, however, is partial at best, and may not last.

And on June 13, 2010, Secretary General Amr Moussa of the Arab League toured Gaza for the first time since Hamas took control there. Moussa, the highest-ranking Arab diplomat to visit in three years, entered Gaza from Egypt through the newly opened border and immediately called for lifting the blockade.

Where was the Arab League for the last three years? Until the Freedom Flotilla, the 22-member group did not speak out seriously against the siege.

Surely the Arab countries, where the people feel so deeply the 60 years of Palestinian repression and the siege of Gaza, would be the logical place to organize flotillas to break the blockade. However, most Arab regimes are in the vest pocket of Wall Street and fear that any show of mass sentiment in their countries could result in their own overthrow. Flotillas from their countries would not be tolerated.

Turkey's contradictions

Meanwhile, Turkey's popularity among the peoples of the Middle East has skyrocketed following its denunciations of Israel's tactics and because it let the flotilla organize from its shores and provided political support. Turkish flags and posters of Prime Minister Recep Tayyip Erdogan have been prominent in demonstrations around the world protesting the Israeli commando attack.

When Israel attacked a Turkish ship in the flotilla, eight of the flotilla participants killed by Israeli commandos were Turks and the ninth was a Turkish American. Turkish Foreign Minister Ahmet Davutoglu, who called for an international investigation, dismissed Israel's proposed panel. He said, "We have no trust at all that Israel ... will conduct an impartial investigation."

There are contradictions here. Turkey, a key U.S. client, was one of the earliest regimes to recognize the Israeli state after it displaced Palestine. However, the Turkish government is strongly against the siege of Gaza and often speaks out against it.

While this view reflects the strong feelings of the Turkish people and plays well for Turkey's domestic audience, the Erdogan government is also seeking some international autonomy.

U.S. wars in the Middle East have hurt the Turkish economy. Turkey has not been admitted to the European Union. So Turkey is striking out more on its own, politically and economically, wanting trade and better relations with Middle Eastern neighbors such as Iran and Syria, which Washington has branded "terrorist."

South African trade unions call for boycott of Israeli apartheid

Unions in Britain and Sweden shun Israeli goods

If I were to change the names, a description of what is happening in the Gaza Strip and the West Bank could describe events in South Africa.
— Archbishop Desmond Tutu, December 1989

Modeled on a similar call by people's organizations in South Africa during the struggle to end apartheid there, on July 9, 2005, 171 organizations representing Palestinians in the occupied territories, the diaspora, and within Israel issued a call for governments, corporations, learning institutions, individuals and trade unions to impose economic measures against Israel. This Boycott, Divestment and Sanctions campaign initiated by virtually all of Palestinian civil society demands that these measures be taken against Israel until it (1) ends the "occupation and colonization of all Arab lands" and dismantles the apartheid wall on the West Bank, (2) recognizes the "fundamental rights of the Arab-Palestinian citizens of Israel to full equality; and (3) respects, protects and promotes "the rights of Palestinian refugees to return to their homes and properties as stipulated in United Nations General Assembly Resolution 194." The 2010 events concerning the Gaza Freedom Flotilla gave a major impetus to this movement.

Published June 16, 2010

Israel and its apologists bristle when Israel is called an apartheid state. Most loudly shouting "Israeli apartheid," however, are those who know the best—the workers of South Africa, who suffered the most under South African apartheid. South African trade unions have denounced the siege of Gaza and the apartheid wall on the West Bank, and have urged forward the Boycott, Divestment and Sanctions campaign (BDS).

Adding their voices to the call to boycott goods from Israel are UNITE, the biggest trade union in Britain, and the Swedish Port-workers' Union, which called a boycott of all Israeli ships and cargo from June 15 through June 24.

The South African Transport and Allied Workers' Union, which refuses to handle Israeli goods at South African ports, called the Swedish boycott "the kind of powerful workers' action that was used during the fight against the South African apartheid regime and helped bring it down. It must be used again today against this criminal apartheid regime in Israel."

The South African Municipal Workers Union announced June 4 that it would "engage every single municipality to ensure that there are no commercial, academic, cultural, sporting or other linkages what-soever with the Israeli regime. ... Every SAMWU branch will immediately approach municipal and water authorities to become part of the BDS campaign, and to publicly declare their solidarity with the Palestinian people."

The Congress of South African Trade Unions expressed outrage at the May 31 killing of activists by Israeli commandos, and in a statement urged "all South Africans to refuse to buy or handle any goods from Israel or have any dealings with Israeli businesses." This umbrella group of unions supports "the inalienable right of the Palestinian people to national sovereignty" and demands "the immediate end to the Israeli siege and the illegal occupation of the sovereign territory which has been violently seized from the Palestinian nation."

Biggest British union joins boycott

UNITE, Britain's biggest trade union, just voted for a complete boycott of Israeli goods and services at its annual conference in Manchester. The 2-million-member union called Israel a "terror" state, with "a policy of ethnic cleansing." UNITE said it would "actively and vigorously" promote a boycott of Israeli goods and services "similar to the boycott of South Africa during the apartheid era," and also pursue a policy of divestment from Israeli companies.

Other labor groups protesting the May 31 Israeli commando raid on the Freedom Flotilla are the International Dockworkers Council, the International Transport Workers Federation, the International Trade Union Confederation, the South African National Union of Mineworkers, the Canadian Union of Public Employees and the British Trade Union Congress. The British University and College Union broke ties with the Histadrut, a Zionist so-called labor organization. UCU spokesperson Tom Hickey said the Histadrut "supported the Israeli assault on civilians in Gaza" and "did not deserve the name of a trade union."

San Francisco dockworkers honor picket, won't unload Israeli ship

By Judy Greenspan
Oakland, Calif.
Published June 23, 2010

When an Israeli cargo ship pulled into Berth 58 in the Port of Oakland on the evening of June 20, 2010, there were no dockworkers on hand to unload it. Longshore workers refused to cross a picket line of hundreds of labor and community activists protesting Israel's blockade of Gaza and its recent murderous attack on the Gaza Freedom Flotilla.

The day had begun at 5 a.m. at the West Oakland BART station. Members of the Labor/Community Committee in Solidarity with the Palestinian People had gathered before dawn to march to Berth 58, where an Israeli ship from the Zim shipping line was due to dock. By 5:30 a.m., a loud, organized, roving picket of hundreds of people had blocked all four entrances to the Port of Oakland berth.

The chants of "Free, free Palestine, don't cross our picket line" were heard throughout the port area. Truck drivers making early morning deliveries to Berth 58 blew their horns and refused to cross the picket line. At 7 a.m., the first shift of dockworkers drove up and, one

Queers Undermining Israeli Terrorism (QUIT) pickets Israeli ship.

WW photos: Judy Greenspan

by one, drove back home, honoring the strong protest.

The picket line continued into the late afternoon and successfully turned away the second shift of dockworkers, who also honored the picket line and returned home.

Members of International Longshore and Warehouse Union, Local 10, were out on the picket line all day talking to protesters and showing their support for the action. Clarence Thomas, an ILWU lineman and leader, thanked the Labor/Community Committee and the San Francisco and Alameda County Labor Councils for their support of this action.

Both labor councils recently passed resolutions criticizing Israel's attack on the Gaza Freedom Flotilla and demanding that Israel lift the blockade of Gaza. Thomas called today's picket line "historic" and "reminiscent of the 1977 action on Easter Sunday," when dockworkers conducted a one-day job action to protest the massacre of South Africans in apartheid Soweto. Thomas noted that dockworkers around the world, in South Africa, Norway and Sweden, have declared that they will refuse to handle any Israeli cargo.

In a short interview with this reporter, Thomas talked about the 1984 organizing effort by progressive ILWU members that led to an 11-day work stoppage and boycott to protest South African apartheid. "Our actions helped raise the level of resistance to apartheid in this country, especially among workers," Thomas stated. "This protest today will also help raise consciousness among longshore workers about the need to end the Israeli blockade of Gaza," Thomas added.

The protest was endorsed by a broad coalition of progressive organizations, including Arab-American Union Members Council, Al-Awda, the Palestine Right to Return Coalition, Answer, Palestine Youth Network, International Action Center, Transport Workers Solidarity Committee, and many other labor and community organizations in the Bay Area.

U.N. report says Flotilla activists were 'killed execution style'

Published Oct. 1, 2010

Israeli naval commandoes intercepted and attacked the humanitarian Freedom Flotilla, aimed at breaking the blockade of Gaza, on May 31. Eight Turkish activists and one Turkish-American were killed on board the Mavi Marmara, a Turkish ship, which was in international waters.

Israeli forces "gravely violated international humanitarian and human rights laws" when they attacked this aid flotilla, according to the United Nations Human Rights Council's fact-finding mission in a report issued Sept. 22, 2010.

The report revealed that forensic evidence showed that 19-year-old Turkish-American Furkan Dogan and five Turkish citizens were killed execution-style by the Israeli commandos.

The Turkish government gave the autopsy report on Dogan, a U.S. citizen, to the U.S. government in July. Nothing was done nor has the U.S. press reported this.

The scathing 56-page report puts the blame squarely on Israel for the fatal commando assault. It said that the Israeli military's conduct "towards the flotilla passengers" showed "unnecessary and incredible violence" and "an unacceptable level of brutality. Such conduct cannot be justified or condoned on security or any other grounds." (UN.org, Sept. 23)

The report cited "clear evidence" of violations of the Fourth Geneva Convention, including "willful killing, torture or inhuman treatment and willfully causing great suffering or serious injury to body or health."

The report strongly recommends prosecution for violations of international law. Israel must provide "prompt" and "adequate compensation" to "those who suffered loss as a result of the unlawful actions of the Israeli military," said the panel.

It also called the situation in Gaza a "humanitarian crisis" and said the blockade of Gaza is "totally intolerable and unacceptable." While Israel claims to have eased the blockade, many essential goods are still not allowed into Gaza. Residents are not allowed to freely exit or visitors to enter, including relatives.

The U.N. panel criticized the Israeli government for not cooperating with its inquiry. Israel has opposed any independent investigation into the lethal raid and held its own bogus inquiries in the face of international criticism.

The report will be presented to the 57-member U.N. Human Rights Council.

The big-business-owned U.S. media has barely covered the news of this report.

.

XI

Military-Industrial-Media Complex 'Rewrites' the Gaza War

$1,300 a second in profits trumps the truth about Palestine

By Joyce Chediac

Fairness and Accuracy in Reporting, the main U.S. media-watch organization, charges that the country's two top newspapers, after the attack by Israel on ships bringing aid to Gaza, suddenly "mis-remembered" what had happened earlier in the 2008-2009 Gaza war. FAIR says the *New York Times* and the *Washington Post* "propagated an inaccurate historical context that serves to bolster Israel's claims." (June 21, 2010)

These newspapers are the most prestigious in the country. The *New York Times* sets the news agenda for the rest of the media.

What did they do?

Throughout the coverage of Israeli's May 31, 2010, attack on the Gaza Freedom Flotilla, during which Israeli commandos killed nine people, these newspapers repeated as fact Israel's bogus claims that it had begun its three-week onslaught on Gaza in December 2008 because Hamas was firing rockets into Israel.

Before the Gaza war, however, both newspapers had debunked this claim. A Dec. 19, 2008, *New York Times* article by Ethan Bronner reported that Hamas had been "largely successful" in seriously curtailing rocket fire from Gaza. "Hamas imposed its will and even imprisoned some of those who were firing rockets," wrote Bronner. An editorial in the Nov. 2, 2008, *Washington Post* said that, thanks in part to "a cease-fire deal with Hamas, Israel has been more peaceful in recent months than it has been in years."

FAIR said, "Part of Israel's strategy of defending its attack on the humanitarian flotilla has been to stress the dangers posed by Hamas rule in the Gaza Strip." By taking it upon themselves "to rewrite relevant history," the "*Times* and *Washington Post* gave this Israeli government argument credibility."

A look at the casualty figures for the three-week war reveals where the "danger" really came from. The Palestinian jurists' organization al-Haq reported that the Israeli military killed more than 1,400 Palestinians, 83 percent of them civilians, including 355 children. In those three weeks a total of 13 Israelis died. Four were killed by Palestinian rockets, three of them civilians. An additional nine Israeli soldiers were killed in Gaza, four of them by Israeli "friendly fire," according to the Israeli government.

Other major media who 'forgot'

The *Times* and *Washington Post* were not the only major media to conveniently "forget" the facts behind Israel's punishing onslaught on Gaza and warp them to provide justification for Israel's later killing of nine people on ships delivering humanitarian aid to Gaza. FAIR also cites CNN, USA Today, Fox News, NBC Nightly News, the *Los Angeles Times*, the *San Francisco Chronicle* and the *Dallas Morning News* for media rewrites of the Gaza war.

These media, FAIR says, downplayed Palestinian civilian deaths, the anguish of the survivors and the suffering caused by the destruction of Gaza's infrastructure. They covered the deaths as merely "a public relations problem for Israel." They also denied that an ongoing humanitarian crisis had been created by the bombing and blockading of Gaza. These newspapers, television networks and radio shows even blamed the Palestinian organization Hamas for Israel's destruction of Gaza. (fair.org media advisories of January and March 2009)

While the establishment media occasionally report the real details of Israeli aggression against the Palestinian people, this coverage is sporadic at best. There is certainly no consistent attempt to be "fair" or to "give both sides." On the contrary, the real relationship of forces— repeated, unprovoked Israeli aggression versus Palestinian measures of self-defense—if reported on at all, is quickly dropped by all the corporate media for a revision of history favoring the Israeli regime and vilifying the Palestinians. This revision is repeated again and again, at all levels of the media.

Israeli lobby doesn't 'control' U.S. media

Why has it been nearly impossible for the Palestinian people to get fair coverage in the establishment media? Some say it is because Jewish people or the Israeli lobby "control" or "unduly influence" U.S. media outlets. But this is not the case. The real force behind this biased reporting is the huge aggregate of U.S. corporations that pull in mind-boggling profits from exploiting Middle East resources.

ExxonMobil, for example, the wealthiest company in the world, with important Middle East holdings in oil and natural gas, had revenues of $477 billion in 2008. (*CNNMoney*, Jan. 30, 2009) It is only one of the U.S. oil giants operating in the Middle East. Meanwhile, Israel's entire gross domestic product that same year was $205 billion. (*CIA World Factbook*)

The oil companies and other U.S. corporations are calling the shots and the Israeli state works for them. What is Israel's job? To be a watchdog for the oil companies.

Soon after the establishment of Israel, one of its most important newspapers wrote that "strengthening Israel helps the Western powers maintain equilibrium and stability in the Middle East. Israel is to become the watchdog. There is no fear that Israel will undertake any aggressive policy towards the Arab states when this would explicitly contradict the wishes of the U.S. and Britain. But if for any reason the Western powers should sometimes prefer to close their eyes, Israel could be relied upon to punish one or several neighboring states whose discourtesy to the West went beyond the bounds of the permissible." (*Ha'aretz*, Israel's newspaper of record, Sept. 30, 1951)

These U.S. corporations don't mind if Israel is blamed for the anti-Arab bias in the U.S. media establishment. It hides their own role. The corporate media help obscure the real relationship of forces.

Bamboozling the public

The major media are welded to this corporate network in what has become a military-industrial-media complex. The media's "job" is to keep the U.S. public from seeing that a few individuals and corporations reap billions of dollars by exploiting the people of the Middle East and bombing and blockading Gaza. These super-rich hate and fear the national liberation struggles, especially the Palestinian struggle, because the Israeli state, which ousted and replaced Palestine, serves U.S. finance capital so well.

The corporate media have a profit motive, too. They get ads and financial sponsorship from giant corporations. They have interlocking directorates with oil, arms and other companies that profit from Middle East occupations and wars. They use their vast conglomerates of newspapers, magazines, networks and entertainment companies to promote a political climate that favors profit-taking while censoring out news that interferes with that. The big media eagerly self-censor if it furthers their burning cause—making more money.

In 2008 ExxonMobil made $1,300 in profits every second. For the military-industrial-media complex, this trumps the truth about Palestine.

Media monopoly: big five control it all

"We have no obligation to make history. We have no obligetion to make art. We have no obligation to make a statement. To make money is our only objective."

When Michael Eisner wrote these candid words (in what he thought would remain an internal memo), he was CEO of the Walt Disney Co. The quote appears in the documentary "Mickey Mouse Monopoly—Disney, Childhood & Corporate Power." The Disney Co. is the second-largest media giant but brings in the largest revenue of any media conglomerate in the world.

The corporate media say they are committed to "report the truth" and that they "strive to be fair" or at the very least "tell both sides." This is as much spin as the *New York Times* and *Washington Post* rewriting the Gaza war. The media are corporations. Like every other corporation, they are in business to make money.

At the end of World War II, 80 percent of the daily newspapers in the U.S. were independently owned. Today, only five giant companies—Time Warner (CNN, AOL), Disney (ABC), Rupert Murdoch's News Corporation (Fox), Bertelsmann of Germany (the world's biggest publisher of English-language books), and Viacom (formerly CBS)—control most of the television, radio, magazines, newspapers, books, movies, videos, music, photo agencies and wire services people in this country rely on. General Electric's NBC is a close sixth. (*The New Media Monopoly*, Ben Bagdikian, Beacon Press, 2004)

These media monopolies are truly huge. Time Warner, the biggest, has 292 separate companies and subsidiaries. The Walt Disney Co.

owns eight book publishing imprints, the ABC-TV network has 10 owned and operated stations, 30 radio stations, 11 cable channels, 13 Internet broadcasting channels that operate around the world, 17 Internet sites and more. The other media giants have similarly large holdings.

The extent of this monopolization is well hidden. But the truth is that "a shrinking number of large media corporations now regard monopoly, oligopoly and historic levels of profit as not only normal, but as their earned right," says Bagdikian.

Sumner Redstone, head of Viacom and owner of CBS, MTV, BET and Paramount Pictures, explains how conglomerate media profit-taking works: "When you make a movie for an average cost of $10 million and then cross promote and sell it off of magazines, books, products, television shows out of your own company, the profit potential is enormous." (*Rich Media, Poor Democracy: Communication Politics in Dubious Times*, Robert W. McChesney, University of Illinois Press, 1999)

In bed with the biggest corporations

The giant corporate media are not a "free press." They are a press happily married to the pursuit of profits. The "freedom" they pursue is the freedom to make a buck. These profits are only partially earned via big media's hundreds of subsidiaries. Even more important is the money to be made through the mainstream media's interlocking relationship with even larger monopolies.

About 118—that's the number of people who sit on the boards of directors of the 10 biggest media giants. These 118 individuals in turn are on the corporate boards of 288 national and international corporations. And eight out of 10 big media giants share common memberships on each other's boards of directors. ("Big Media Interlocks with Corporate America" by Peter Phillips, Common-Dreams.org, June 24, 2005)

This integration occurs at the very pinnacle of corporate power. For instance, board members of ABC/Disney, NBC/GE, CBS/Viacom, CNN/TimeWarner, Fox/News Corp., *New York Times* Co., *Washington Post/Newsweek*, *Wall Street Journal*/Dow Jones, Tribune Co., Gannett and Knight-Ridder also sit on the boards of 13 of the Fortune 500's 25 most profitable companies and probably have indirect connections to the other 12. This linkage forms a huge matrix of interlocking corporations and monopolies, usually with banks at the center, that control the U.S. and to a large extent the world economy.

'Enhancing values preferred by corporate world'

"The dominant media firms, now among the largest in the world, have the power and use it to enhance the values preferred by the corporate world of which they are a part," says Bagdikian. This includes self-censorship, based upon class and financial interests, or "omission of the news that might interfere with the media's maximizing their own profits. The same tendency makes the news media sympathetic to similar profit maximization by whatever means among corporations in general."

This is what is passed off as "objective reporting" to 310 million people in the U.S.

At the same time, with each new round of consolidations, the media as a whole has moved more openly to the right. For example, the right-wing-and-proud-of-it Fox News, with 23 wholly owned or affiliated network stations in the U.S., is the fourth-largest television network, right behind ABC, CBS and NBC.

Corporations benefit from vilifying Palestinians

Which corporations benefit the most from vilifying the Palestinian people and their leaders?

Far above all others, it's the oil and energy companies, which also pull in the greatest profit.

ExxonMobil and Chevron, the first- and second-largest U.S. oil companies, top the Fortune 500 list. ExxonMobil reported the highest annual profit in corporate history in 2006. The next year it broke its own profit record, clearing $40.61 billion or nearly $1,300 a second. (CNNMoney, Feb. 1, 2008) As of July 1, 2010, ExxonMobil occupied eight out of the 10 slots for the largest quarterly corporate earnings of all time and five out of the 10 largest annual corporate earnings slots.

Chevron and Conoco, the second- and third-largest of the U.S. oil giants, are not far behind.

While these oil companies drill, pump and refine all over the world, their profit empires rely most of all on control of the cheap, easily extracted, high-grade oil in Saudi Arabia, Kuwait, Qatar, the United Arab Emirates and, once again, in Iraq. They were also in Iran until the revolution of 1979 kicked them out and nationalized the oil. They vowed to never let this happen again.

ExxonMobil sees Palestinian rights as a threat to "their" profits of $1,300 a second. With these warped values prevailing, the Palestinian people don't stand a chance of fair coverage in the corporate media.

Chevron, Washington, *New York Times*: one voice

In 1944, when the U.S. was becoming the dominant power in the Middle East, the U.S. State Department described Middle Eastern oil as "a stupendous source of strategic power, and one of the greatest material prizes in world history."

Washington's assessment of that area has not changed.

"The Middle East, with two thirds of the world's oil and the lowest cost, is still where the prize ultimately lies," said Dick Cheney. This was in 1999, when he was still CEO of Halliburton, the world's second-largest provider of equipment and services to oil and gas companies. Cheney was George H. W. Bush's secretary of defense before his stint at Halliburton and later became George W. Bush's vice president. This is not a coincidence.

"Cheney once drew parallels between his role as CEO of Halliburton and his role as secretary of defense. Addressing the Gulf Coast Association of Geological Societies convention in Corpus Christie in 1998, he stated: "In the oil and gas business, I deal with many of the same people." (CorpWatch, July 25, 2000)

Understanding the needs and wants of the oil companies is a big plus for those aspiring to high government office, since Washington safeguards these needs and wants. Condoleezza Rice prepared for her roles as George W. Bush's national security advisor and then secretary of state by first representing an oil company. She was on Chevron's board of directors and even headed the oil giant's committee on public policy.

Oil companies also mesh with the huge Pentagon apparatus that protects them. Currently on Chevron's board is Donald Rice, who was Bill Clinton's secretary of the Air Force from 1989 to 1993.

The media monopolies are not far behind, as many have interlocking directors with Big Oil. General Electric (NBC) interlocks with Mobil, CNN with Chevron, Knight-Ridder with Phillips Petroleum, the *New York Times* with Texaco (whose parent company is Chevron). And some "public" television news shows are connected to Big Oil through ad revenues. Chevron is a key funder of the most influential show on PBS, the nightly "News Hour with Jim Lehrer." (FAIR, Dec. 19, 2007)

This is why Washington officials, Chevron and the *New York Times* speak with one voice.

A military-industrial-media complex

Oil companies are not the only U.S. corporations making money hand over fist. Arms sellers are awash in profits. In 2005, for example, the top military contractors had a record $25 billion to $30 billion in cash in their coffers. Lockheed Martin, the largest arms seller in the world and the biggest supplier of weapons to Israel, topped the list. (*New York Times*, May 12, 2005)

There is an incestuous relationship between Big Oil, the weapons makers and the media. Oil companies want a strong military presence in the Middle East to protect them from the people whose resources they exploit. In addition, the military machine that protects oil company interests is itself the largest consumer of oil in the world. And because the media monopolies interlock with both, they are in on the take when both make profits.

How does the military exert its influence on the media?

For one thing, the big media welcome ads from the weapons makers. Lockheed Martin is a major advertiser on CNN, which is owned by Time-Warner. Boeing is a major funder of PBS's "Washington Week."

Some media are actually owned by arms merchants. NBC's parent company is General Electric. GE Aviation makes the propulsion systems found on U.S. aircraft sold to the Israeli Air Force, including the F-16 Fighting Falcon and F-4 Phantom, the CH-53 heavy-lift helicopter, the "Apache" attack helicopter and UH-60 Black Hawk utility helicopter, as well as the Israeli-made Kfir fighter plane. Some of the attack helicopters GE outfits are used in the occupied territories. GE also makes parts for Hellfire II laser-guided missiles as well as T-700 and 701C jet engines used by the Israeli Defense Forces (IDF). (Seattle Palestine Solidarity Committee)

So when reporters, analysts and guest "experts" at NBC find excuses to justify Israel's attack on Gaza, they don't mention that their salaries are paid by a company that makes a mint providing the very weapons that Israel used. NBC doesn't make a cent from exposing the terrible toll these weapons have taken.

Another way the arms makers influence the media is through corporate interlocks with media companies that weld together their interests.

This relationship between media and the military has become such a fixture that it is an integral part of the for-profit capitalist system. Normon Solomon explained that "a military-industrial-media complex ... now extends to much of corporate media. ... Often, media magnates and people on the boards of large media-related corporations enjoy close links—financial and social—with the military industry and Washington's foreign policy establishment." (Norman Solomon, *War Made Easy: How Presidents and Pundits Keep Spinning Us to Death*, Wiley & Sons, 2005)

What has this meant for reporting?

"By the time of the 1991 Gulf War, retired colonels, generals and admirals had become mainstays in network TV studios during wartime. Language such as 'collateral damage' flowed effortlessly between journalists and military men who shared perspectives on the occasionally mentioned and even more rarely seen civilians killed by U.S. firepower."

In Gulf War 'the press wanted to be used'

Solomon continued: "News coverage of the Gulf War in the U.S. media was sufficiently laudatory to the warmakers in Washington that a former assistant secretary of state, Hodding Carter, remarked (C-Span, 2/23/91): 'If I were the government, I'd be paying the press for the kind of coverage it is getting right now.'"

A media insider who covered the 1991 Gulf War for the *New York Times* later wrote, "The notion that the press was used in the war is incorrect. The press wanted to be used. It saw itself as part of the war effort." (Chris Hedges, *War Is a Force That Gives Us Meaning*, Anchor Press, 2003)

The corporate media also see themselves as "part of the war effort" that Israel is waging against Gaza.

Bombing Gaza: 'sweet deal' for arms makers and media

Frida Berrigan, a senior research associate at the World Policy Institute and co-author of the report "U.S. Military Assistance and Arms Transfers to Israel," said in an interview: "So you have maybe 10 weapons corporations in this country that have a stake in—essentially in Israel using its military arsenal so that it can be replenished again." ("Democracy Now," Pacifica Radio, July 21, 2006)

The Council for a Livable World Education Fund says most U.S. aid is for the military, while 90 percent of all U.S. foreign aid goes to the

Middle East. Like the oil companies, the arms makers are dependent on Middle East business for their huge profits.

Israel is the largest recipient of this aid, at $3 billion yearly.

Egypt ($2 billion a year) is the second-largest recipient, with Saudi Arabia not far behind. These Arab regimes are hated by their own people because they are U.S. clients. They are as unstable as a house of cards and the Pentagon lives in constant fear that they will be overthrown. At the same time, U.S. arms makers can't resist "dumping" weaponry on oil-rich Arab client regimes, obliging them to use their petrodollars to buy overpriced U.S. weaponry. For example, in the 1980s, Saudi Arabia paid $6 billion for Boeing AWAC spy planes, despite the restriction that they be flown only by U.S. pilots.

Israel is different. This European settler state is the only regime in the area that Washington feels it can really rely on to strike against the people of the Middle East without major ramifications back home. This is why Israel is treated very differently than the Arab regimes by the U.S. government and corporations, including the corporate media.

U.S. taxpayers foot bill for Israel's weapons

Israel doesn't pay for its weaponry. Most of the money "given from the United States, from U.S. taxpayers, to Israel is then spent on weapons from Lockheed Martin and Boeing and Raytheon. [Israel goes] straight to U.S. corporations with U.S. money to buy weapons that are then used in the Occupied Territories and against Lebanon." (Frida Berrigan)

The U.S. gives the Israeli military sophisticated high-tech weapons that it will give to no other government. U.S. arms makers have joint ventures with Israeli weapons makers. And Israel is the only regime that uses these U.S. weapons regularly and in a big way—against the Palestinians and other Middle Eastern people.

Who are these U.S. weapons makers arming Israel, and how do they connect to the media?

Boeing: provided small-diameter bombs dropped on Gaza

Boeing is the world's largest aerospace and defense company, with annual sales of $61.5 billion. According to Indymedia Corporate Watch for 2009, Boeing was involved in sales to Israel of 42 AH-64 "Apache" fighter helicopters and 18 newer AH-64D "Apache" Longbow fighter helicopters, 63 F-15 Eagle fighter planes, 102 F-16, F-16 II and F-16 III fighter planes and four Boeing 777 commercial planes, as well as AGM-

114D Longbow Hellfire missiles and Arrow and Arrow II interceptors developed in collaboration with Israel Aircraft Industries.

In 2008, the U.S. government approved the sale of 1,000 Boeing GBU-9 small-diameter bombs to Israel, in a deal valued at up to $77 million. Since each of these bombs weighs only 250 pounds, aircraft can carry more of them and therefore attack more targets. They were dropped on Gaza.

The Disney Co. (ABC) has a direct link with Boeing.

Lockheed Martin: F-16 jets and guided missile system used in Gaza

Lockheed Martin, with sales in 2008 of $42.7 billion, is the world's largest weapons contractor. It makes the Hellfire precision-guided missile system, reportedly used in Gaza. Israel also has 350 F-16 jets, some purchased from Lockheed Martin. The F-16 is considered the most sought-after fighter plane. Israel's fleet is the largest outside the U.S. (Indymedia Corporate Watch, 2009)

Lockheed Martin has a $4-billion deal to co-produce with the Israeli military a version of the F-16 fighter plane called the Sufa (meaning "storm" in Hebrew). Production begins near Tel Aviv and is finished in Fort Worth, Texas. (Frida Berrigan)

Lockheed Martin has interlocking directors with the *Washington Post* and Gannett.

Caterpillar: delivered the bulldozer that killed Rachel Corrie

With more than $30 billion in assets, Caterpillar is the world's largest maker of construction equipment. It is one of scores of U.S. companies that are technically not weapons makers but whose products are links in the chain that makes Israeli aggression possible or especially devastating.

Caterpillar makes the D9 military bulldozer, designed for use in invasions of built-up areas. Since 1967, Israel has used these bulldozers to destroy tens of thousands of Palestinian homes and uproot hundreds of thousands of trees.

The D9 bulldozer was extensively used by Israel in its 2001-2002 Operation Defensive Shield attack, particularly during the invasion of the West Bank town of Jenin, where countless homes were destroyed by bulldozers and a disabled man was crushed to death.

Caterpillar has profited from the construction of the West Bank apartheid separation wall. U.S. activist Rachel Corrie was run over and murdered by an Israeli soldier driving a Caterpillar D9 bulldozer in 2003 as she tried to stop it from destroying a Palestinian home in the Rafah refugee camp in Gaza.

Caterpillar interlocks with the Tribune Company, owner of the *Chicago Tribune* and the *Los Angeles Times*.

Raytheon: No profits in peace
Raytheon, with annual revenues of $20 billion, supplies electronic equipment for the West Bank apartheid wall. Since 1998, Raytheon has sold Israel more than 200 AIM-120 Advanced Medium Range Air-to-Air Missiles at a total cost of more than $100 million, as well as 14 Beech King B200 fixed-wing aircraft for $125 million and a Patriot missile system for $73 million, according to the Federation of American Scientists.

Raytheon made the 100 bunker-buster bombs flown by the U.S. to Israel at the height of the bombardment of Lebanon in 2006. (Counterpunch, May 28, 2008) These weapons were also used in Gaza.

This company makes the "Tomahawk" missile, the Sidewinder and other high-tech missiles that Israel has in its arsenal. These missiles have very sophisticated, heat-seeking targeting components that interface with GPS. (Frida Berrigan)

Raytheon is jointly marketing one of these missiles, the Black Sparrow ballistic target missile, with the Israeli weapons maker Rafael. Raytheon's program manager for this project, Adam Cherrill, actually advocates further expansion of "Greater Israel" and believes Israel has "a far stronger claim to Judea and Samaria, which is considered the West Bank, than the Arabs." (Counterpunch, Feb. 11, 2003)

This might seem like Cherrill has been "unduly influenced" by Israel. The wars against Arabs that follow from this view, however, would bring billions in profits to Raytheon. After all, weapons are made to be destroyed, and then to be ordered again. For weapons makers, there are no profits to be made in peace. Raytheon has an interlocking director with the *New York Times*.

U.S. companies make the profits, Israel makes the kill
The media have developed selective amnesia when it comes to the Palestinian people because, like all corporations, they are drawn to greater profits like a moth to the flame. U.S. companies make the profits when Israel makes the kill.

The corporate media are in on the killing. They use their vast communication fleets to bombard the population here with fiction that confuses people and disarms them politically. By finding ways to justify Israeli aggression, they help pave the way politically for the next Israeli attack on Palestinians.

Media-industrial-military behemoth has soft underbelly

But this corporate media empire cannot fool all the people all the time. Its weak underbelly is that it underestimates the power of a people united and determined to resist. All the weapons in the U.S. arsenal couldn't bomb Gaza into submission. Gaza still stands strong and its resistance has inspired solidarity from millions of people. Many of these people are also fighting for their own rights, often against the very same corporations that profit from Gaza's anguish.

Another weakness of the corporate media is that the World Wide Web and other forms of instant communication they dominate can be used by the Palestinian people and those in solidarity with their struggle. Through online blogs, posting photos and YouTube videos, Facebook, Twitter, e-mails and texting, activists have provided instant coverage of their solidarity trips, their reception in different countries and the conditions in Gaza.

Palestinians from the Occupied Territories have spoken directly to U.S. demonstrations via satellite cell phones. Freedom Flotilla videographers have posted their footage of the Israeli commando raid on the web.

There is a people's media that is breaking the ABC, CBS, NBC and FOX blockade of the truth. They will not be stopped.

From the People's Media:

Who was Furkan Dogan?

A study of Associated Press media coverage in 2004 revealed that the news service "reported prominently on Israeli deaths at a rate 2.0 times greater than Palestinian deaths. In reality, 7.6 times more Palestinians were killed than Israelis in 2004. ... Palestinian children were being killed at a rate over 22 times greater than Israeli children. ... Israeli children's deaths were covered at a rate 7.5 times greater than Palestinian children's deaths."
—*If America Only Knew Media Report Card Study,* made by ifamericaknew.com/media during the second Palestinian intifada

Furkan Dogan was 19 when he was killed by Israeli commandos seizing the humanitarian Freedom Flotilla in international waters on May 31, 2010. Dogan was born in New York State and raised in Turkey. He was the only U.S. citizen killed in the Israeli assault. Usually when people from the United States are killed abroad in assaults, their pictures appear in the papers and the stories of how they were killed are told. Their local congressperson, and sometimes even the president, send condolences to the family. At the very least, the media interview the family. None of this happened here. Furkan Dogan's short life and violent death were ignored by the politicians and censored out of the U.S. media.

An example of the people's media that is challenging this monopoly on news is this excerpt from the blog of Ralph Loeffler. Loeffler lives in New Jersey and participated in the Viva Palestina 5 convoy that broke the blockade of Gaza in October 2010 by bringing in humanitarian aid. Loeffler's full blog can be found at the site of the International Action Center (iacenter.org). There are many blogs like his on the web.

Gravesite of Furkan Dogan.   Photo: Ralph Loeffler.

Blog of Ralph Loeffler, Oct. 5, 2010

Furkan Dogan. I'm going to say Furkan Dogan so often that it will seem as "American" as Tom Smith or Bill Jones. Furkan Dogan was an American, a young American of only 19 years, when on May 31st a hail of Israeli bullets ended his life on the Gaza aid ship Mavi Marmara.

Furkan was filming the Israeli assault when an IDF commando fired his first shot pointblank, hitting Furkan squarely in the head. Four more shots were fired into Furkan, leaving him dead and unrecognizable. Furkan, who was born in the Albany-Troy area of New York, had gone back to live in his family's hometown of Kayseri, Turkey. His family knew the names of the Turks that had been killed on the Mavi Marmara but one casualty had not been immediately identified. In their normal pattern of lies and misinformation the Israelis had not identified Furkan because he was an American. They waited until the initial impact of their murderous attack on innocent humanitarians subsided a bit before confirming the ninth victim was Furkan.

When Furkan's father went to meet the Mavi Marmara's survivors and casualties, he had no idea that his son had been murdered. Instead of greeting his son he was taken to the morgue to identify his remains. Surely such a day defies description; I won't attempt one.

The Viva Palestina 5 convoy arrived in Kayseri late on September 29th and spent the night on a mountain overlooking Kayseri. We had come to Kayseri for the sole purpose of visiting Furkan's gravesite and extending our condolences to his family. The following morning we were told that our convoy would be passing by the high school from which Furkan had graduated and that students from the school would be waiting for us. As we began our slow journey down the twisting mountain road, the convoy took on the air of a funeral procession.

Suddenly, there they were. The students lined both sides of the road, standing for who knows how long. Each one sadly, silently, proudly held up Furkan's picture as the convoy rolled by.

Beautiful, moving words were spoken at the gravesite and afterwards we met with Furkan's family at the recently built community center named after Furkan. The grandfather and uncle bore their grief, perhaps with the acceptance of mortality that comes with age. But the older brother's grief was palpable. Deep, dark lines were etched under his eyes and he seemed to be disconnected to his surroundings. Never have I seen such pain expressed on a human face.

Any country should be proud to have a promising young man such as Furkan as one of its own. Intelligent and mature beyond his years, Furkan had already dedicated his life to the struggle for Palestinian justice. Such a course bears no import with the U.S. Congress, which rubberstamps the U.S. funding of the occupation. The Israeli thug who gunned down Furkan is no more responsible for murdering him than Furkan's own country, which paid for the bullets.

XII

Moving Forward

To fully understand events in Gaza, this small strip of land and the people who live there must be seen in the broader historical and geopolitical context. In this chapter are four selections.

Two messages from the Palestinian people view Gaza in the larger Palestinian context to answer the questions "What do Palestinians want?" and "How can supporters best help?"

By writing "Free Gaza and Palestine" on a Warsaw Ghetto wall, an Israeli war resister takes back Jewish history of the Holocaust from the Zionist distortion and puts it in its rightful place, beside the world's oppressed people.

A leader in the U.S. movement to free Palestine analyzes the connection between Palestine, Israel and the U.S., and details how Israel's attacks on liberation movements in the Mideast help the U.S. government keep its stranglehold on Middle Eastern oil profits.

'We must free all of Palestine'
A message from the Palestinian people

*The movement in solidarity with Gaza has grown significantly since
Operation Cast Lead and the Israeli commando attack on the Gaza
Freedom Flotilla. Where is this movement going?*

*Lamis Deek, speaking for Palestinian individuals and organizations in
the solidarity movement, described the direction Palestinians would like to
see this movement take. Deek is co-chair of Al-Awda NY, The Palestine Right
to Return Coalition. She made her remarks at a June 17, 2010, meeting in
New York reporting back from the Gaza Freedom Flotilla.*

"We want to ask, where is this movement going?

"My biggest fear as this movement grows is that it will not end justly,
that the Palestinians will end up in ghettos in a land that we call
Palestine filled with Bantustans where Palestinians are divided from
each other.

"We in the Palestinian movement ask our friends to be conscious of
this when we move forward, and to join the movement for Palestinian
liberation ... there is a clear political direction that will see a proper and
just solution to the injustices that we see perpetrated by Israel today and
over the last 62 years. ...

"The nine volunteers who were killed by Israel commandos when
they seized the Gaza Freedom Flotilla ... died not simply trying to deliver humanitarian aid to Gaza, but really to tell the story of Palestine. ...

"In 1948 Zionist control of Palestine and surrounding Arab lands
was cemented. ... It was at that point that two-thirds of the Palestinian
population was exiled and made refugees. And to this day they are
continuously exiled."

Deek referred to the "extreme Judaization of Jerusalem and in
Nablus" on the West Bank today, where Jewish settlers, under the
direction and protection of the Israeli government, continue an
aggressive theft of Palestinian land. There are apartheid laws that
Palestinians live under in Haifa, and other parts of what is called Israel.

She explained that it is clear to the Palestinian people that their conditions have gotten much worse since the 1993 Oslo Accords, and its attempts to confine a Palestinian state to only the West Bank and Gaza.

"When Palestinians voted for Hamas, they weren't just voting for an Islamic government. In fact, many of those who voted for Hamas were Christians. They were voting for full resistance to Israeli occupation and one Palestinian state in all of Palestine…

"Our call is simple. It is a call to be treated as equals on all levels, on the economic, on the social, on the political, on the human level; for full equality with the rest of humankind; the right to return and remain in their homes in dignity; the right to live without restrictions, the right to visit our sisters and brothers in Syria and Lebanon and Egypt, the right to be reunited as one part of the Arab world as it was before 1948, for one democratic state in all of Palestine."

Jewish people must accept equality of Palestinian people

She called on Jewish people "to accept justice and repatriation of the Palestinians to their rightful homes, [to] accept the idea of Palestinians as equal human beings."

Deek called for "the full dismantlement of all the Zionist structures, all the Zionist laws, all the Zionist institutions and the repatriation of every single Palestinian refugee and their descendants, and reparations for every Palestinian and their descendants.

"Under those conditions we will have full equality—and not Jewish supremacy, which is what we have in Israel, what we have in the occupied Palestinian lands—one democratic state where all human beings, Palestinian and Arab, Christian and Jewish, are treated as equals.

"That is the message moving forward, from the Palestinian people and from Palestinian organizations here."

'Support a campaign addressing all forms of Palestinian oppression'

The following statement was made by Al-Awda NY, The Palestine Right to Return Coalition, on June 23, 2010.

In the year and a half since Israel's massacres in Gaza, the Palestine solidarity movement, for 15 years weakened by the two-state "Peace Roadmap" of the 1993 Oslo Accords, has gone through what can only be described as a major political recalibration.

After years of meaningless "peace negotiations," the aim of Oslo—a "Jewish state" on 78 percent of historic Palestine and a rump "Palestinian state" on the remaining 22 percent—is rapidly losing whatever credibility it may have once had among Palestinians. Indeed, outside the Palestinian Authority, created by Oslo to serve Israeli interests, it is hard to find any Palestinian voices advocating for such a solution with conviction.

From the ruins of Oslo have emerged new campaigns with holistic goals. The most significant of these has been the Boycott, Divestment and Sanctions (BDS) movement, initiated and overwhelmingly supported by Palestinian civil society.

San Francisco   WW photo: Judy Greenspan

This campaign seeks to address the entire spectrum of what BDS leader Omar Barghouti describes as Israel's "three-tiered system of oppression against the Palestinian people": the 1967 occupation of Gaza, the West Bank and East Jerusalem; the denial of Palestinian refugees' right of return; and the systemic discrimination against Palestinian citizens of Israel.

These BDS demands present a direct challenge to the Zionist regime of Jewish domination over the Palestinian people. The same goals have generated growing support for the principle of a single, democratic state throughout all of historic Palestine. Even longtime two-state supporter Mustafa Barghouti concedes: "I believe the vast majority of Palestinians would accept equal rights and one person, one vote in one state with alacrity. I certainly would were we to reach such a day."

Outrage over Israel's atrocities in and against Gaza—including the recent assault on the Gaza Freedom Flotilla—has dramatically infused these ideas into the international Palestine solidarity movement, thrusting the Palestinian struggle in the world spotlight as perhaps never before. Despite attempts of its opponents to tar it with the brush of anti-Semitism, BDS is increasingly advocated throughout the world, often by Jewish activists.

Zionist organizations have noted these developments with alarm. The Reut Institute, a leading Israeli think tank, recently warned that support for BDS is based on a "set of ideas that are increasingly sophisticated, ripe, lucid and coherent," which, if not aggressively countered, could lead to a "paradigm shift from the Two-State Solution to the One-State Solution as the consensual framework for resolving the Israeli-Palestinian conflict."

Meanwhile, some in the solidarity movement seek to limit or even oppose BDS. They claim that it is "unrealistic," or even morally undesirable, to advocate BDS goals that challenge the separate "Jewish state" envisioned by the "Two-State Solution." Although those who argue this include courageous critics of Israeli policy, their position here is deeply flawed.

First, the principle of self-determination means, above all, that decisions about what is or is not "realistic" belong to those who live under oppression, rather than their sympathizers—however well meaning. "As in the struggle against South African apartheid," writes Omar Barghouti, "genuine solidarity movements recognize and follow the lead of the oppressed, who are not passive objects but active, rational subjects that are asserting their aspirations and rights as well as their strategy to realize them."

Second, is there any social justice movement that has not seemed "unrealistic" or even impossible? Yet circumstances change rapidly and unpredictably; what was fantasy yesterday often comes true tomorrow. It is enough to remember the long decades that preceded the abolition of slavery, the civil rights victories of the 1960s, or the collapse of colonialism and apartheid in southern Africa.

Third, the "Two-State Solution" is itself realistic only as ratification of a fractured, Israeli-controlled Bantustan: a "Two-Prison" solution, as Palestinian activist Haidar Eid bluntly describes it. This has been the Israeli and U.S. goal since the beginning of the "peace process"; indeed, anyone looking to catch a glimpse of a future Palestinian "state" need look no further than the systematic strangulation of Gaza and continued "Judaization" of the land on both sides of the 1948 "Green Line." In that sense, the most dangerous aspect of this solution is precisely that it is possible.

Finally, "pragmatism" at the expense of justice is always an illusion. As Martin Luther King Jr. famously pointed out, true peace is not merely the absence of tension, it is the presence of justice. An apartheid state built on the notion of Jewish supremacy in an Arab land cannot be part of that vision of justice; on the contrary, it promises unending oppression and conflict.

Although it would be naive to expect an imminent collapse of this state, the genie is out of the bottle. If King was right—that the arc of the "moral universe" does indeed bend toward justice—there is reason to be confident about the movement's long-term prospects.

Now more than ever, it is time for the solidarity movement to align itself with the growing number of Palestinians in the 1967 occupied territories, the refugee communities, and within the 1948 lands calling for a single democratic Palestinian state of all its citizens from the river to the sea.

This cannot happen until all those and their descendants who were driven from their villages and cities in 1948 by terror, force and massacre are able to return and live in freedom and equality in all of historic Palestine. For those interested in true peace, that is the only pragmatic option.

'Israelis need liberation from the crimes of their government'

By Michael Kramer
Published July 19, 2010

On June 27, 2010, Israeli military resister Yonatan Shapira and Polish activists from the Palestine solidarity organization Kampania Palestyna sprayed a remnant of the Warsaw Ghetto wall with the words "Liberate All Ghettos" in Hebrew and "Free Gaza and Palestine" in English. They then hung a Palestinian flag from the wall.

Warsaw Ghetto uprising

The wall that surrounded the Jewish Ghetto in Warsaw was built in 1940 when Poland was occupied by German fascists, the Nazis. Hundreds of thousands of Jews, as well as smaller numbers of Romani people, were imprisoned in the Warsaw Ghetto before they were transported to the Auschwitz and Treblinka extermination camps. In April 1943 a heroic armed uprising began in the ghetto and lasted for one month before being put down by the German Army. The ghetto was then completely leveled, yet some fighters were able to hold out for months in underground bunkers.

Israel distorts history of the Holocaust

Ewa Jasiewicz, a Pole who participated in the Gaza Freedom Flotilla and was part of the June 27, 2010, action at the wall, said, "Poland is full of the ruins of ghettos and death camps and shrines to those who sacrificed their lives in the defense of not just their communities but in resistance to fascism."

Like Gaza, the Warsaw Ghetto was a symbol of terrible oppression and incredible resistance. But Israel has tried to distort the history of the Holocaust and events at the Warsaw Ghetto, raising a hysteria that Jewish people live in constant danger of this happening to them again to justify its oppression and brutality against the Palestinian people, who had nothing to do with these events in Europe, and only seek to return to their homes in Palestine.

By inscribing the plight of Gaza and Palestine on the Warsaw Ghetto wall, these activists have reclaimed the Warsaw Ghetto Uprising, placing it where it rightly belongs, firmly on the side of the oppressed and persecuted against the world's oppressors, including the Israeli state.

Former pilot who refused to target Palestinians

Yonatan Shapira, the Israeli military resister who participated in the action, was a captain in the Israeli Air Force. He flew U.S.-made Black Hawk helicopters in the same unit that was to take part in the May 31, 2010, attack on the Gaza Flotilla ship Mavi Marmara.

In 2003 Shapira wrote a letter refusing to take part in missions targeting Palestinians. It was co-signed by 27 other Israeli pilots. That was the end of his military career.

Since then he has become a well-known activist who supports Palestinian self-determination and the Boycott, Divestment and Sanctions movement. He is a co-founder of Combatants for Peace, an organization of former Palestinian and Israeli armed combatants.

Descendant from Polish Jews killed in death camps

Shapira explained, "Most of my family came from Poland and many of my relatives were killed in the death camps during the Holocaust. When I walk in what was left from the Warsaw Ghetto, I can't stop thinking about the people of Gaza who are not only locked in an open-air prison but are also being bombarded by fighter jets, attack helicopters and drones, flown by people I used to serve with before my refusal in 2003. ...

"I was always taught growing up that the atrocities that happened to the Jewish people happened because the world was silent. And therefore I cannot be silent. The Jewish people needed to be liberated from the ghettos, and now Israelis need to be liberated from the crimes of their own government.

"Each of us can take part in this global struggle for justice and support the Boycott, Divestment and Sanctions movement for the sake of not just the Palestinian people but for Israelis, too." (www.kampania-palestyna)

Palestine, Israel and the U.S. in a global perspective

The following excerpts are from a talk by Bill Doares at the Workers World Party National Conference, Nov. 14, 2009.

No people on earth have been more attacked and vilified by the U.S. ruling class and its media than the people of Palestine and the Arab and Islamic world in general.

In the 61 years since they were driven from their homes by European settlers who called themselves "Israelis," the Palestinian people have been occupied, massacred, bombed, imprisoned and called "terrorists and fanatics" for simply wanting to go home, for wanting to live in peace and freedom in their own land.

For 61 years, the racist apartheid settler state called "Israel," erected on the ruins of their towns and villages, has been supplied with an endless stream of dollars and sophisticated weapons of mass destruction by both Republican and Democratic administrations.

Look at Gaza, where we traveled in July with the Viva Palestina medical aid convoy: this small island of freedom that is at the same time the biggest prison on earth. A small sliver of land where 1.5 million Palestinian women, children and men are denied food, medicine and the right to travel by an international conspiracy between the U.S., Israel, Western Europe and U.S.-allied Arab regimes; an array of forces not unlike that faced by revolutionary Haiti in 1804 or the workers of Paris in 1871.

U.S. Congress blocked action on U.N.'s war crime report

Look at the rain of U.S.-made bombs and missiles unleashed on Gaza in December 2008 and January 2009, a slaughter that even the U.N.'s Goldstone Commission was forced to condemn as a war crime, and look how the U.S. Congress and administration rushed to condemn and block any action on that report.

Look how former U.S. Congresswoman Cynthia McKinney was kidnapped at sea by Israeli commandos for trying to bring aid to the people of Gaza, and both the White House and the U.S. media were completely silent about this brazen act of international piracy. All because the Palestinians of Gaza dared to practice democracy, to cast their votes for Hamas, a party that refuses to relinquish the Palestinian people's Right to Return.

Strategic role of Mideast oil to U.S. empire

What crime have Palestinians committed? Like the people of Iraq and Afghanistan, of Somalia and Iran, they were born in a region that holds three-fifths of the known reserves of oil, the world's most profitable commodity, a region that corporate America must keep oppressed and divided.

Arab and Iranian oil once provided 60 percent of the overseas profits of the Fortune 500; it made ExxonMobil, BP and ChevronTexaco the richest companies on earth. Today the same Wall Street bankers who plunder the U.S. Treasury while throwing workers out of their homes suck trillions of dollars in tribute from the corrupt feudal regimes of the Arabian Peninsula. The big arms contractors depend on sales to that part of the world.

But any Arab regime could be swept away by the people as suddenly as the Shah of Iran was in 1979. Instead of enriching Wall Street bankers, their oil wealth could build schools and hospitals, as it did in Iraq before the U.S. invasion, as it has done in Iran since 1979 or is doing in Venezuela today. It could provide the material basis not only for an independent, unified Arab nation but also for an ALBA-type alliance of the entire African-Asian region.

U.S. general calls Israel 'unsinkable aircraft carrier'

To maintain its obsolescent position at the center of the global capitalist economy, the U.S. capitalist class can only rely on force and destruction. Israel is nothing but a giant U.S. military base dividing Asia from Africa, a loaded gun pointed at the Arab people, an "unsinkable aircraft carrier" in the words of Alexander Haig, Ronald Reagan's secretary of state.

In the words of Hugo Chávez, "Why was the state of Israel created? ... To divide. To impede the unity of the Arab world. To assure the presence of the North American empire in all these lands."

When the Palestinian people demand their right to return home, they not only challenge U.S. control over the entire region. They raise an issue that shakes the very foundations of monopoly capitalist power:

the fundamental right of a dispossessed people to take back what was stolen from them. This is the right the people of Zimbabwe and South Africa are also fighting for. It is the right of Native and Black and Mexicano people in this country, of workers whose homes and jobs have been stolen by the banks.

The cause of Palestine is the cause of the workers and oppressed everywhere.

Contributing writers

Abayomi Azikiwe is editor of Pan-African News Wire, an electronic press agency founded in 1998. He has worked for decades in solidarity with liberation movements and progressive governments on the African continent and in the Caribbean. He is co-founder of several Detroit-area organizations: Detroit Coalition Against Police Brutality, Michigan Emergency Committee Against War & Injustice, and Moratorium NOW! Coalition to Stop Foreclosures, Evictions and Utility Shut-offs. A broadcast journalist for 12 years, Azikiwe has hosted and co-hosted programs on WHPR Radio in Highland Park, Mich.; WCHB, WDTR and WDTW in Detroit; and CKLN in Toronto. He recently launched a weekly two-hour blog talk radio program entitled "Pan-African Journal." His articles have been published in the Zimbabwe *Herald*, the *New Worker* in England, the *Michigan Citizen*, *Africa Insight* in South Africa, the Center for Research on Globalization in Toronto and *Workers World*, where he is a contributing editor.

John Catalinotto was civilian organizer for the anti-war, anti-racist American Servicemen's Union from 1967 to 1971. He has been a managing editor of *Workers World* newspaper since 1982. He edited two books, *Metal of Dishonor* about depleted uranium use in Iraq (1997) and *Hidden Agenda: the U.S.-NATO Takeover of Yugoslavia* (2002). An organizer for the International Action Center Tribunal on Iraq (August 2004), he also represented the IAC at the Tribunal on Israeli War Crimes against Lebanon (February 2008). He has coordinated international communications for joint protests before the 2003 war against Iraq and for protests of the 2006 Israeli aggression against Lebanon and the 2008-2009 Israeli attack on Gaza. Catalinotto is a lecturer in mathematics at City University of New York.

Joyce Chediac traveled to Libya in 1987 following the U.S. bombing of that country. She witnessed the first Palestinian Intifada in 1988 in the West Bank and Gaza Strip. In 2009 Chediac visited Lebanon to observe conditions of Palestinian refugees there and the reconstruction of Lebanon, organized by the resistance following the 2006 Israeli bombing. Her works include "The massacre of withdrawing soldiers on 'The Highway of Death'" in Ramsey Clark et al., *War Crimes: A Report on United States War Crimes Against Iraq* (Maisonneuve Press, 1992). Her articles in *Workers World* include: "Munich 1972: What Spielberg left out" (Feb. 16, 2006); "A tale of two crises: Lebanon rebuilds, New Orleans waits" (Aug. 23, 2006); "'Right of return' still key demand after 61 years in Lebanon" (Oct. 17, 2009); and "U.S. occupation increased violence against Afghan women" (Aug. 26, 2010). Chediac is a school nurse.

Dolores Cox is an International Action Center volunteer, member of the New York Free Mumia Abu-Jamal Coalition, and contributing writer to *Workers World* newspaper. She is a retired New York City social worker and a union member for over 35 years. Cox says: "As an African American, I've witnessed and experienced the daily oppression of U.S. Black communities in a country ruled by racist, white-supremacist ideology. I see the connection between the crimes against humanity committed by U.S. imperialism and terrorism worldwide, and by Israel and the U.S. throughout Palestine. My activism is largely centered around the intertwining of the struggles of all oppressed people for liberation and justice, for their right to resist and to self-determination. I stress the need for educating, organizing and providing mutual support."

Bill Doares is a lifelong Palestine solidarity activist. He was New York City coordinator of the Viva Palestina USA-Lifeline 2 convoy that brought medical aid to Gaza in July 2009 and works with the International Action Center and Al-Awda NY, The Palestine Right to Return Coalition. As a teenage member of Youth Against War and Fascism in the late 1960s and early 1970s, he helped organize some of the first rallies and teach-ins for Palestine in the U.S. Doares helped found the November 29 Coalition for Palestine, later the Palestine

Solidarity Committee, in 1981. He was one of seven U.S. activists arrested on false charges and expelled from Palestine by the Israeli state during the First Intifada in 1988. He organized New York City protests against the Israeli attack on Gaza in December 2008 and January 2009. Most recently, he was coordinator of the Sept. 11, 2010, Emergency Mobilization against Racism and Anti-Islamic Bigotry, which defended the Islamic community center in lower Manhattan. A union member since 16, he took part in organizing drives at a shipyard, a hospital and a television plant in Virginia in the 1970s and was for two decades a delegate and negotiating team member in the Communications Workers of America.

LeiLani Dowell is a managing editor of *Workers World* newspaper. She traveled on a fact-finding delegation to Lebanon after the Israeli bombing and invasion of 2006 and reported back on the devastation she observed. Dowell is a student and a national leader in Fight Imperialism, Stand Together (FIST). She was a Women's Fightback Network delegate to a women's anti-imperialist conference in Montreal in August 2010. In 2004, she was a Peace and Freedom Party candidate for Eighth Congressional District in San Francisco. She is also an activist in the lesbian, gay, bi, trans and queer movement.

Sharon Eolis is a retired emergency room nurse and family nurse practitioner who describes herself as an anti-racist, anti-Zionist Jewish woman who has organized in solidarity with Palestine since the June 1967 war. Eolis helped organize the manifest list of medical supplies delivered to Gaza by the July 2009 Viva Palestina USA Lifeline 2 convoy. She traveled to Iraq in 1998 and 2000 with the Iraq Sanctions Challenge, bringing more than $1 million in medicine and other aid, and coordinated and provided health care for both Iraq delegations. She is a contributing author to *Challenge to Genocide: Let Iraq Live* by Ramsey Clark et al. Eolis was a New York State union delegate with United American Nurses. As grievance chairperson at Cabrini Medical Center in New York City, she opposed racist practices by management and verbal racist attacks by patients on health care workers of color.

Shelley Ettinger is an anti-Zionist Jew and longtime activist in support of the Palestinian struggle. She initiated an appeal by Jews in Solidarity with Palestine in January 2009 and wrote the statement excerpted in this book. Ettinger, a union member for over 30 years, was a leader of strikes by public transit workers in Ann Arbor, Mich., and clerical workers at New York University. She co-founded the Lesbian and Gay Labor Network and co-chaired the first LGBT-labor solidarity rally at AFL-CIO headquarters.

Sara Flounders is co-director of the International Action Center, an activist organization opposing U.S. war and racism. Her article "The tunnels of Gaza: An underground economy and resistance symbol," received an award by Project Censored and was included in its top 25 most-censored stories of 2009. She has twice visited Palestine and has written and spoken on the difficult conditions she witnessed, especially in Gaza. She is a co-editor and contributing writer to several books, including: *Metal of Dishonor—Depleted Uranium: How the Pentagon Radiates Soldiers & Civilians with DU Weapons* (1997), *NATO in the Balkans: Voices of Opposition* (1998), *Challenge to Genocide: Let Iraq Live* (1999) and *Haiti: A Slave Revolution* (2004), all published by the International Action Center.

Judy Greenspan is a third-grade public school teacher in Richmond, Calif. She is a member of both Workers World Party and Al-Awda, The Palestine Right to Return Coalition, and is a long-time activist in the struggles against racism and occupation. In 2009, she traveled to Gaza with the Viva Palestina USA Lifeline 2 convoy and helped to successfully break the blockade for one day in order to deliver needed medical and other humanitarian aid. Greenspan was a founder of the California Coalition for Women Prisoners and a leader of California Prison Focus, having spent 20 years fighting for prisoners' rights and health care for those behind bars.

Deirdre Griswold is editor of *Workers World* newspaper. Her support for the Palestinian struggle dates back to the 1967 war, when as a leader of Youth Against War & Fascism and editor of *The Partisan* she published many articles supporting the Palestinian struggle. Griswold spent six months in 1967 working on the London Secretariat of the 1967 Bertrand Russell International War Crimes Tribunal exposing U.S. crimes in Vietnam. Griswold was Workers World Party's first presidential candidate in 1980. Her many works include *Indonesia 1965: The Second Greatest Crime of the Century* (World View Publishers, 1970); *The Ethiopian Revolution and the Struggle Against U.S. Imperialism* with Sam Marcy et al. (WVP, 1978); and "How U.S. destroyed progressive secular forces in Afghanistan," *Workers World*, Sept. 27, 2001. She co-edited the book *Low-Wage Capitalism: What the new, globalized high-tech imperialism means for the class struggle in the U.S.* by Fred Goldstein (World View Forum, 2008).

Dee Knight was, from 1968 to 1975, co-editor of *Amex-Canada*, the newsletter of U.S. war resisters in exile during the U.S. war against Vietnam. In that role he worked from 1973 to 1977 with Vietnam Veterans Against the War and others to found the National Council for Universal and Unconditional Amnesty and served on the NCUUA national board during those years. He has organized and written for the past three decades in the GI resistance movement and is a frequent contributor to *Workers World* newspaper.

Michael Kramer was a member of the Israeli Defense Forces and took part in the 1973 Arab-Israeli War. His personal experiences both as a settler and combatant led him to reassess his views on Zionism and the role of the U.S. in the Middle East. Kramer became a supporter of Palestinian self-determination and the Arab cause. He is a member of Veterans for Peace and an elected officer of Chapter 021 (Northern New Jersey).

Cheryl LaBash is a Workers World Party national organizer and a co-coordinator of the U.S.-Cuba Labor Exchange, frequently visiting Cuba and Mexico to facilitate this annual worker-to-worker conference. She also speaks on behalf of the Michigan Campaign to Free the Cuban Five, five Cuban heroes imprisoned in the U.S. She is an organizer for the Detroit-based Bail Out the People Movement and a former construction inspector for the city of Detroit.

Ralph Loeffler is a social justice activist who does volunteer work with the International Action Center in New York City and the Viva Palestina charity in Britain. Since July 2009 he has participated in three land convoys with Viva Palestina which delivered hundreds of vehicles and millions of dollars in emergency aid to the Israeli-besieged Gaza

Strip. His efforts with the International Action Center have focused on opposition to the wars in Iraq and Afghanistan. Prior to his retirement, Loeffler worked for almost 30 years for a financial services company.

John Parker is West Coast coordinator of the International Action Center. He was the press secretary for the July 2009 Viva Palestina USA Lifeline 2 convoy. In 1998, after Sudan's main pharmaceutical plant was demolished by a U.S. missile strike, Parker went on a fact-finding trip to that country and has written and spoken about what he saw. Parker visited Iraq after the first Gulf war of 1991 and then spoke at meetings across the U.S. on the terrible effects of sanctions on the civilian population there, especially on children. He was part of a U.S. delegation to Iran in October 2010 to build international anti-war solidarity. Parker was the presidential candidate of Workers World Party in 2004. As a leader in the Los Angeles anti-war movement, he helped organize and chair several large rallies against the U.S. war in Iraq. Parker chairs the Central Area Neighborhood Council in South Central Los Angeles.

Betsey Piette is a coordinator of the International Action Center in Philadelphia and a contributing editor to *Workers World* newspaper. A leader in the Philadelphia anti-war and Palestine solidarity movement, she has helped organize protests in support of the people of occupied Palestine and is on the board of Playgrounds for Palestine. She has participated in international delegations to Colombia and Venezuela. Piette is also an organizer with International Concerned Family and Friends of Mumia Abu-Jamal and writes extensively on his case.

Acknowledgments

All the labor that made this book possible was voluntarily provided by people who believed in the book, many of whom made sacrifices to make it happen.

Thanks to Paul Wilcox and Naomi Cohen for their critical reading of the first draft. Thanks to Lal Rookh for her strong and moving cover design. Thanks to Dee Knight for producing the book singlehandedly and also helping to promote it. Thanks to Frank Neisser for designing and putting up the web page: GazaResistanceBook.com. Thanks to Paul Teitelbaum and Janet Mayes for indexing the book.

Thanks to the staff of *Workers World* newspaper who edited, proofed and fact-checked the pieces in this book, and special thanks to *WW* Editor Deirdre Griswold for her style and proofing expertise, her 19-hour proofing marathon and her good advice.

Thanks to Sara Flounders, who multi-tasked to produce and promote this book as only she can, and special thanks to staff volunteers who proofread, fact-checked, did fundraising, worked with the printer, and fretted until everything was right.

Very special thanks to those who opened their pockets to provide the seed money to publish this book, many contributing more than once.

Finally, and most importantly, we are deeply in debt for this book to the Palestinian people — in the West Bank and Gaza, living in what is now called Israel, and in the Diaspora. Your determination to resist for more than 60 years never ceases to inspire, and to teach the world that all is possible

Index

W★RKERS WORLD

We live in a world of fake news. The corporations and big banks that own this so-called media plot overtime to make sure we don't get the truth and fight back. *Workers World* is a different kind of newspaper. Our voices are not those of the status quo or the system's defenders. In WW, you find the voice of workers and oppressed people who strive for a different world in which no one is held down by the chains of exploitation, racism, sexism or anti-LGBT bigotry.

Workers World is able to publish anti-war, anti-racist news because we are truly independent.

Subscribe to *Workers World* weekly newspaper
workersworld.net
workers.org

Follow Workers World on Twitter
http://twitter.com/workersworld
Facebook http://bit.ly/c4ndYg

Low-Wage Capitalism

Fred Goldstein

Colossus with feet of clay:
What the new globalized high-tech imperialism
means for the class struggle in the U.S.

Low-Wage Capitalism

What the new globalized high-tech imperialism means for the class struggle in the U.S.

An easy-to-read analysis of the roots of the current global economic crisis, its implications for workers and oppressed peoples, and the strategy needed for future struggle.

"In this period of economic uncertainty, Fred Goldstein's *Low-Wage Capitalism* could not be better timed. Beautifully written, deeply considered and backed by impressive research, this is essential reading for anyone wishing to understand the true nature of the world we live in and the factors that have led to so much turmoil. ... Urgently recommended."
Gregory Elich,
author of *Strange Liberators*

"We need to get this book into the hands of every worker. It clearly explains the capitalist economic threat to our jobs, our pensions and our homes. But, even more importantly, it shows us how we can fight back and win!"
David Sole, President, UAW Local 2334, Detroit, Michigan

"With the capitalist system demonstrably unfair, irrational, and prone to intermittent crises, it is useful, indeed refreshing, to see a Marxist analysis of globalization and its effects on working people. Fred Goldstein's *Low-Wage Capitalism* does exactly that."
Howard Zinn, author of
A People's History of the United States

"*Low-Wage Capitalism* by Fred Goldstein is a most timely work, as the working class prepares for a fightback during the greatest crisis of capitalism since the Great Depression."
Clarence Thomas, ILWU Local 10 and Co-chair, Million Worker March Movement

"*Low-Wage Capitalism* is truly outstanding, hits us like a body punch, and provides the perfect context for what we all need to know about the evolving conditions of workers and their struggles. ...
Deserves the widest readership."
Bertell Ollman, author and Professor of Politics, NYU

"Patriarchal prejudice serves capitalism in two ways: it keeps the whole working class divided, and it holds down wages for women and for lesbian, gay, bisexual, and transgendered workers. *Low-Wage Capitalism* shows the necessity and the great potential for solidarity among all the low-wage workers of the world."
Martha Grevatt
Nat'l Executive Officer Pride At Work, AFL-CIO, UAW Local 122

"Lucid, deeply accurate and informative, as relevant and useful as a book can be, Goldstein offers a compelling analysis of the exploitative world of global corporate capitalism. ..."
Michael Parenti,
author of *Contrary Notions*

"160 years after the publication of the *Communist Manifesto*, Fred Goldstein takes on the challenge of applying Marxist political economy to the burgeoning crisis of capitalist globalization in the 21st century. ..."
Abayomi Azikiwe, Editor,
Pan-African News Wire

"From the point of view of Filipino workers in the U.S., the largest exploited and abused Filipino workforce outside the Philippines ... we are pleased with the exposé of imperialist globalization as the main culprit of global forced migration. ..."
Berna Ellorin,
Secretary-General, BAYAN USA

"This book helps us to understand the root of the present neoliberal globalization— a new stage of the international capitalist crisis—which was imposed by U.S. imperialism and which devastated Latin American economies. ..."
Ignacio Meneses,
Co-chair, U.S.-Cuba Labor Exchange

World View Forum paperback, 2008, 336 pages, pages, charts, bibliography, index

The author is available for lectures and interviews.

Review online at
LowWageCapitalism.com

HIGH TECH, LOW PAY
A Marxist Analysis of the Changing Character of the Working Class
By Sam Marcy, Second Edition with a new introduction by Fred Goldstein

With an introduction by Fred Goldstein, author of **Low-Wage Capitalism**

Twenty years ago Marcy wrote that the scientific-technological revolution is accelerating a shift to lower-paying jobs and to more women, Black, Latino/a, Asian, Arab and other nationally oppressed workers.

Using Marxism as a living tool, Marcy analyzes the trends and offers strategies for labor, including the occupation of plants.

A new introduction by Fred Goldstein, author of *Low-Wage Capitalism*, explains the roots of the current economic crisis, with its disastrous unemployment, which has heightened the need for a working-class resurgence.

World View Forum paperback, 2009, 156 pages, charts, bibliography, index

Books available online at **Leftbooks.com** and on sale at bookstores around the country.

Rainbow Solidarity

In Defense of
CUBA

By Leslie Feinberg author of
Stone Butch Blues

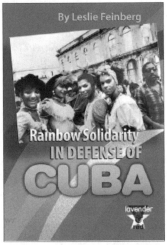

By Leslie Feinberg

Rainbow Solidarity in Defense of Cuba documents revolutionary Cuba's inspiring trajectory of progress towards liberation of sexualities, genders and sexes.

This ground-breaking book reveals how the Cuban Revolution has grappled with the pre-revolutionary legacy of 450 years of persecution and exploitation of homosexuality.

Rainbow Solidarity answers the demonization of the 1959 Cuban Revolution by Washington and the CIA, Wall Street and Hollywood by demonstrating that the process of solving these problems is the forward motion of the revolution.

Today, after decades of concrete efforts and achievements—together with free health care and education, and jobs and housing for all— Cubans enjoy freedoms regarding same-sex love, transsexuality and gender expression in Cuba that don't exist in the imperialist United States.

World View Forum paperback 2008, 116 pages, photos, bibliography, index

 Rainbow Solidarity in Defense of Cuba is an edited compilation of 25 articles from the *Workers World* newspaper series by Feinberg entitled Lavender & Red, online at www.workers.org

First public event for Rainbow Solidarity for the Cuban Five at the New York City LGBT Community Center in June 2007. Secretary Jorge Luis Dustet from the United Nations Cuban Mission he holds up poster with the names of the first 1,000 signers of the call for Rainbow Solidarity with the Cuban Five.

The Cuban Five are Gerardo Hernández Nordelo, Ramón Labañino Salazar, Rene González Sehwerert, Antonio Guerrero Rodríguez and Fernando González Llort, political prisoners held in U.S. prisions.

MARXISM, REPARATIONS
& the Black Freedom Struggle

An anthology of writings from *Workers World* newspaper.
Edited by Monica Moorehead. Includes:

**Racism, National Oppression
and Self-Determination**
Larry Holmes

**Black Labor from Chattel Slavery
to Wage Slavery**
Sam Marcy

Harriet Tubman, Woman Warrior
Mumia Abu-Jamal

Black Youth: Repression & Resistance
LeiLani Dowell

**Black & Brown Unity:
A Pillar of Struggle for Human Rights
and Global Justice!**
Saladin Muhammad

**Are Conditions Ripe Again Today?
40th Anniversary of the 1965
Watts Rebellion**
John Parker

Racism and Poverty in the Delta
Larry Hales

The Struggle for Socialism Is Key
Monica Moorehead

**Domestic Workers United Demand
Passage of a Bill of Rights**
Imani Henry

Causes of Turmoil in Jamaica
Pat Chin

**Africa Needs Reparations,
Not Occupation and Sanctions**
Deirdre Griswold

**Black Reconstruction:
The Unfinished Revolution**
Minnie Bruce Pratt

World View Forum 2007, paperback
200 pages, photos

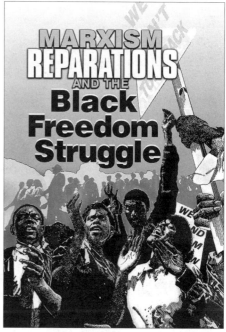

COVER ILLUSTRATION BY SAHU BARRON

"These essays, from a variety of folks working on a number of Black struggles, testify to the central truth that Black History is the epic saga of resistance, rebellion and revolt. These struggles show us all that true freedom is still an objective to be attained, rather than a reality. What, pray tell, did Katrina show us?"

— **Mumia Abu-Jamal**
Political prisoner writing from Pennsylvania's death row. His 6th book published by City Lights Books, 2009
*Jailhouse Lawyers: Prisoners
Defending Prisoners vs. the U.S.A.*
is available at Leftbooks.com.

Books available online at **Leftbooks.com** and on sale at bookstores around the country.

A Voice from Harper's Ferry, 1859
by Osborne P. Anderson, a Black revolutionary who was there.

Also the essays:

The Neglected Voices from Harper's Ferry
Mumia Abu-Jamal

What Is a Nation?
Monica Moorehead

The Unfinished Revolution
Vince Copeland

A unique book from the raid on Harper's Ferry. Few history books give Osborne P. Anderson the recognition he deserves. Anderson was the only Black combatant to survive the raid and to write about it. His account of this turning point in the struggle against slavery—an armed attack by Black and white volunteers on a citadel of the South—refutes those who try to minimize the role of African American people in fighting for their freedom.

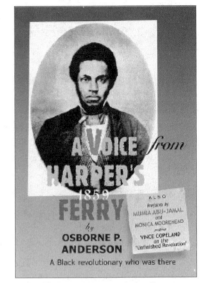

World View Forum paperback,
124 pages, photos

The Prison-Industrial Complex:
An interview with Mumia Abu-Jamal

Monica Moorehead and Larry Holmes interview Mumia—journalist, political activist and wrongfully convicted death row inmate —framed for his ideas. Abu-Jamal speaks on prison labor in the United States, youth, elections, economics and the state of the world.

Also includes articles on:

The Oppressed Nations, the Poor & Prisons
Monica Moorehead

The Death Penalty & the Texas Killing Machine
Teresa Gutierrez

World View Forum, 2000 paperback, saddle stitched, 32 pages, photos

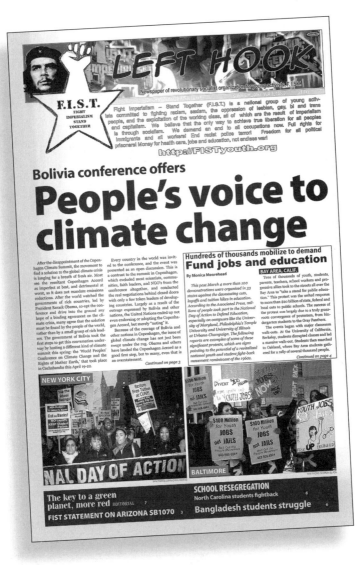

Left Hook is the quarterly newspaper of the revolutionary socialist organization for young activists, Fight Imperialism–Stand Together (FIST). Each edition of *Left Hook* will provide analyses of political events, social movements and revolutionary struggles that impact our world. Commentary, theory, culture, and news reporting intersect in the pages of *Left Hook* to provide readers with radical analysis from a Marxist perspective.

Subscribe to *Left Hook*   2 years: $10.00
http://FISTyouth.org